CMF DESIGN

**The Fundamental Principles of
Colour, Material and Finish Design**

CMF DESIGN

I want to extend my special thanks
to all the people who believed in
my vision and without hesitation,
supported this project with
enthusiasm and meaningful content.

PREFACE

Through several years of professional practice of CMF design, I have received many enquiries from fellow colleagues, design professionals, mentees and students, about where to find a good source of information and reference about the field.

Since CMF design is a rather young discipline for which currently there are no specialized or focused sources of information, I decided to begin consolidating and sharing its key principles. Although it was not always easy to develop clear explanations and practical methods for thinking and doing, little by little my initial compilation of short articles and presentations lead to the creation of this book.

Its content is supported by three main inputs: First, my accumulated professional experience of over 15 years, working internationally with major companies and consumer brands, both as an employee and as an independent consultant; second, it reflects information obtained through a series of expert interviews conducted with professionals with a significant level of experience in the industry and lastly; it presents a number of case studies with innovative companies whom I had the pleasure of personally visit and interview.

I have also had the opportunity to explore these principles in the academic field through different settings involving workshops, independent studies, academic classes and guest lectures at different universities around the world, including Aalto University in Finland, Tama Art University in Japan and Art Center College of Design in Pasadena, California. Throughout this process, the exploration and incorporation of CMF design into current design curriculums has proven to be an important and relevant extension to current practices.

Since CMF design is a broad discipline encompassing different industries, processes and products, the main emphasis of this book is on industrially designed products and industrially manufactured consumer goods, so that the principles presented here are fully supported by actual industry standards and global manufacturing practices.
The final output is envisioned to serve as a canvas for best practices within the discipline of CMF design and is not intended to be a prescriptive formula. Moreover, there can be approaches to the process which vary depending on regional and socio-cultural contexts, aspirational values, type of industry, design field and market dynamics.

Liliana Becerra

**Photo taken at the Lechler Colour Design
exhibition at Fuorisalone 2015 in Milan.**

THE PUZZLE OF CMF DESIGN

When I first approached the task of unwrapping the concept of CMF design, I began by separating and breaking down each of its three components: colours, materials and finishes. As I made progress with my writing and research process, I realized that this classification was actually very difficult to maintain and it became evident that these three elements are impossible to separate from one another.

Every material has its own array of optimal manufacturing processes, which also provide a unique palette of effects. The beautiful shine of an anodised aluminium surface happens only as the result of a thoughtful combination between the reflectivity of the material, the right types of dies, and its unique finishing processes. The hand and colour of a leather piece dyed with natural pigments will be much softer and prone to shifting through time and use, compared to a leather piece dyed with traditional chemical processes

It is impossible to talk about colour without talking about surface detail, texture, reflectivity and overall product composition, all important components of CMF design. A painted colour will become more vivid if applied over a lighter substrate and if coated with a glossy topcoat. A surface with a soft touch finish will make the colour slightly more muted and visually softer. A colour blocking design approach to a product will convey a totally different message to the consumer than a product with a tone-on-tone colour approach.

In most cases the process of CMF design requires a certain amount of experimentation or trial and error, peppered with a healthy dose of observation, curiosity and creativity. Sometimes, the process may start with a material exploration and its subsequent connection to form, surface and colour will follow. In other cases, the colour or technology can become the main innovation to the point of becoming the marketing message itself.

Based on these premises, the concept of CMF design could be approached as a "puzzle of elements" with multiple correct solutions, depending on who is creating it and who it is created for. This does not mean however that CMF design is a random process based on sudden impulse or personal opinions but instead, it confirms that it is and actual science, which should be supported by deliberate professional practice and accumulated real-world experience.

CMF DESIGN

COLOUR DESIGN

CMF

Colour, Material and Finish Design

INTRODUCTION TO CMF DESIGN

Although there are different approaches to the practice of CMF design, which vary according to geographical location, type of industry, level of experience and cultural backgrounds; some fundamental definitions that tend to be common across the board.

WHAT IS CMF DESIGN?

(1) Colour, material and finish design is an emerging professional discipline which focuses on designing and specifying colours, materials and finishes to support both functional and emotional attributes of products. It is an integral process that runs in parallel with the physical and technical design of products. In some industries, it is considered a fundamental part of the industrial design process itself. (2) Identifying the most adequate materials and finishing technologies to ensure the best possible product performance is at the core of CMF design. Only when the perfect balance between visual beauty and functional performance is achieved, can a product provide a consistent and successful user experience.

The work in this discipline combines practical knowledge of functional and technical properties of material technologies with intangible human perceptions of value. (3) Usually, when an object is noticed and picked up upon impulse or curiosity by human hands, it is because its visual appearance, often granted by the CMF design approach, triggers an immediate emotional connection.

(4) Besides the practical and the more intuitive knowledge, there are also external influences that come into to play throughout the CMF design process, such as socio-cultural and aesthetic trends, visual design languages, product categories and early adoption of products by influential consumers groups.

Users can personalize their Jambox Bluetooth speaker with thirteen different grills, nine cap colours and a water resistant coating option.

The smart Brabus tailor made packages offer the possibility to express personal style. Customers can continue the colour scheme from the exterior to the interior with many options for the various parts, leather seats, or even the stitching.

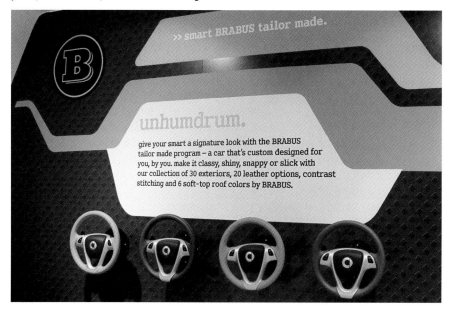

THE INDUSTRY

CMF design is practiced throughout a range of different industries, including apparel, soft goods, consumer electronics, automotive, aviation, cosmetics and packaging for fast moving consumer goods (FMCG).

The demand for CMF design expertise has increased in recent years partly because consumer product manufactures are becoming aware of the great potential in diversifying their product portfolio at a relatively low cost, while still maintaining a similar or the same product shape, functionality or tooling. In this case, CMF design works as a key avenue to create a sense of novelty and higher value propositions within an existing line of products.

From a marketing perspective, CMF design is a valuable tool when it comes to positioning products, collections and categories according to market tiers and consumer segmentations; as it allows for the creation of emotional connections, added value and the fulfilment of certain human aspirations such as beauty and belonging.

Major brands that have succeeded in the market place for a sustained period of time such as Apple, Nike and MINI, as well as newly emerged ones like Jawbone, Beats, and Tesla, advocate for a very well-grounded work on this discipline, often paired with innovative technology development. For these brands, CMF design is a core area of innovation which directly yields into higher brand value and therefore higher profits.

Design-driven organizations with a strong sense of colour and material design normally have dedicated professional teams working in close collaboration with other departments, such as engineering and marketing, in a multi-disciplinary approach, placing product design quality at the core of the process rather than as an after-thought. There are also external and independent individuals and consultancies across the globe whose focus is to advice small and large firms on different areas of expertise within the CMF design discipline.

In the field of interior design and interior architecture the main focus is on large-scale environmental solutions and installations where material and finish choices are expected to last longer and to create bold visual and environmental impact. Since this is a professional discipline with its own line of design principles, requirements and regulations, this book focuses mostly on CMF design for consumer-products and industrially manufactured consumer goods.

THE CMF DESIGN PROFESSIONAL

The CMF design profession is a considerably young discipline that has emerged and consolidated itself during recent years, slowly becoming an independent, well-established design practice and a very sought-after expertise.

Most professionals who work in the field come from a variety of backgrounds and seem to have accumulated their knowledge through hands-on experience. Among the design backgrounds are graphics, textiles, industrial and product design, fashion, apparel, illustration, branding and advertising. As important as the professional experience however, is one's innate sensibility to detect and articulate design languages and aesthetic trends, paired with the ability to understand and translate consumer's aspirations into concrete CMF solutions through engaging storytelling.

There are different professional areas to master within the field of CMF design. All of them are complementary to each other and there is no definite boundary between them. The well-rounded CMF design professional will be versatile in all of them. It is possible however to encounter designers who specialize in some areas more than others.

**Intern Kelley Rother performing
CMF exploration work at MLAb.**

Image courtesy of Suzette Henry, MLAb

 **Colour Design**

This area focuses on designing colour palettes with specific surface finishes. Depending on material properties and on the final product application, there are different ways to achieve colour effects. Part of the colour effect can be the surface finish or the material itself. Most of the work in this area is currently directed to paints and coatings development for automotive interiors and exteriors, or for consumer goods. Besides the technical aspect, the work on colour development requires to be in tune with the ever-changing seasonal market trends.

② Colour Development

This area involves professional exterior and interior paint and finish developers, who have a strong chemistry background. The core activities mostly happen in a lab, mixing of inks and paints in order to create novelty effects with strong technical performance, depending on the industry and the functionality required for the colour. There are companies that specialize only in colour and surface development, serving a range of different industries.

③ Material Design

It generally consists of ideating new and connecting existing material technologies with functional requirements and emerging aesthetic and design trends. In many cases, products with innovative materials instantly become iconic and recognizable within the market place, to the point that

15

material design can become a key element of the brand DNA. Material designers have a strong aesthetic sensibility and an innate curiosity for material exploration, which often leads them to create innovative designs.

 Material Development

This area focuses on creating high-performance materials according to the technical specifications and functional requirements of products. In most cases, materials developers have a strong engineering background or work closely with material engineers. Often, materials developers work in parallel with material designers so that the development can focus more on the technical and functional aspects of the material.

 Surface Design

This area focuses on the design of structures, patterns and graphics, which are then applied to products' surfaces. These include a broad range of natural and synthetic laminates, paper, textiles, carpets and upholstery utilized for home furnishings, apparel, wall coverings, floor coverings and decorative papers – mostly present within in the hospitality and the interior design industry. Although surface design is considered an important part of CMF design, it is also a stand-alone professional discipline for which a corresponding professional degree can be acquired.

Finish Design

This area focuses on designing the final look and feel of products' surfaces with emphasis on manufacturing processes, involving functional and aesthetic characteristics. In most cases, finish design is intrinsic to material design. In fact, some finishes can only be specified according to the material's functional properties or manufacturing possibilities. Since this is one of the building blocks of CMF design, the third part of this

Gathered material samples are displayed on the trend table, aiding in the CMF design ideation and development process.

Image courtesy of Suzette Henry, MLAb

book is dedicated entirely to outline the most common finishing processes according to materials.

CMF Strategy

This aspect oversees all CMF design ideation and development based on marketing and strategic product offering, which usually targets 3 to 5 years out. The professionals working in this area tend to have a strong understanding of consumer insights and are very good at articulating them into concrete product and market opportunities. They are usually long-term visionaries who can be very concrete when it comes to tangible outcomes. This aspect is directly connected with the business side of design since every CMF design offering will be sold and marketed directly to the final consumers.

CMF Development

This area focuses on working closely with vendors in order to develop the specified colours, materials and finishes of products directly for mass-production. Usually this process starts with a target sample, which is then translated technically into a "production usable" material. This is usually a very long process because every sample has to go through an extensive round of approvals, not only in terms of colour, material or finish but also in terms of required technical product specifications. For people working in this area, it is highly recommended to have good organizational skills and some basic knowledge of spreadsheets, in order to successfully track the development, production, approval and overall status of samples.

Trend Tracking and Forecasting

In order to anticipate consumers' wants and needs, CMF designers must anticipate future consumer behaviours and thus, master the ability to forecast emerging trends that will change the market place. Professionals who are experts in this area are very dependable for companies leading the way to the future, as they are able to create scenarios to visualize how products will evolve. Other non-design professionals working in trend tracking and forecasting include futurists and social scientist with a strong consumer insights background.

Storytelling and Marketing

Every CMF designer must be an outstanding storyteller, capable to support and sell ideas to other people both within the company and to the ultimate consumer. Storytelling should not just be based on blue-sky thinking, but on concrete facts and figures to demonstrate why a certain material or a specific colour can increase the consumer appeal and therefore the bottom line in terms of brand value and ultimately profits.

Q&A

SUZETTE HENRY
MATERIAL DIRECTOR MLAB

Suzette Henry started her career in the fashion industry both in sales and merchandising, followed by manufacturing, where she became an expert in sourcing textiles, knits and communicating with vendors at Guess Apparel. She later specialized in denim and opened the first of several material libraries. During her 11 years at Nike, she created the first material design role and opened Jordan's first material library. As the Material Designer for Jordan, her work focused on integrating exclusive colours and materials in hierarchy products, encouraging partnerships for the brand. Currently she is the Material Director of MLab where she has created a unique material resource for Pensole – the first footwear-specific design school in North America. She continues to mentor and open educational opportunities to future Pensole students and design professionals who want to empower their current role, as well as consulting through a colour, material and design lens.

How do you define CMF design from a footwear design perspective?

CMF is about the DNA of materials. You must identify all the aspects you encounter in your design brief. There is the Material ID, which innovates, inspires and solves a problem. Then you have the Consumer ID which describes your consumer and they will be using your product, i.e. geography, lifestyle and price point. Then you need to validate the Performance ID, i.e. how is that material going to be used in the context of testing standards. You also look at the Function ID which specifies whether it is going to be climate sensitive, water proof or water resistant, whether it will have a safety element and how it is supposed to function within design. There is also the Aesthetic ID. It has to inspire but it also has to influence. The aesthetic is really what the consumers see on the shelves and how the CMF design entices them to pick that shoe off the shelf and try it on. Once a person has the garment or the footwear on, 80% of the sale is made – and that is all aesthetics. Then you have the Material Construction ID which details whether it is a woven, a knit, a

① material ID ④ Funtion
② consumer ⑤ Aesthetic
③ performance ⑥ material. construction

micro fibre or maybe coated leather. And the last piece that is also part of the Consumer ID, is whether it is sustainable, whether there is something behind the brand message that makes it validated within a sustainable point of view. Have you provided a compelling product for your consumer to be brand loyal? All of those things to me are what CMF design is about.

Can you name three finishes or material processes specific to the footwear industry?

In footwear, you have a range of finishes that can be applied to a product. These include transparency or translucency, colour shift or spectra flair – which are pigments that are very effective on synthetics because they can give the impression of lightness or refinement. Being able to tell a story using white for consumers in different geography's is easy when you want your product to communicate characteristics like artic, crisp, fractured and structured or, protective, resilient and true. These may not be specific to footwear any longer, because I am aware of automotive trim designers borrowing these cues from footwear. Also currently trending are what we call "low profile packages". These are created by combining a performance base layer – something breathable with stretch and recovery properties – with a foam middle section that adds not only cushion, protection, and aesthetic function but also a colour cue and, lastly, a top layer that is either heat moulded or laminated and provides support and structure. Upper constructions are so much more versatile than just three years ago with the use of packages. This is a huge design tool, as well as branding opportunity.

How is the push for sustainability changing CMF design in the footwear industry?

Sustainability is a huge discipline in footwear and part of almost every seasonal approach. Coming from a Nike background where about 99% of the vendors or suppliers already have a sustainability POV, you are provided with materials that are 100% sustainable in the processes or, for instance in the case of leather, finished through a water-based system. In the design process it is a lot easier to apply sustainability through 3D tools such as "Pattern Cut "or "Knife Cut" that optimize material usage so there is less waste. Sustainability guides how a material is made, how it is going to be used, how it is going to be integrated in the design process and in the brand language.

EMOTIONAL CONTEXT

There are several intangible aspects to the CMF design process. After all, we live in a physical world that we experience primarily through memories and emotional connections.

2

PERCEIVED VALUE

Conveying positive emotions through a sensorial experience can elevate the value of the products. At least 80% of CMF design is about the perceived value it creates for the consumer. Every human being, regardless of ethnicity, social status, education or gender, is looking for aspirational objects to fulfil emotional needs and intangible benefits such as status, beauty and belonging. Creating value through CMF design considers not only the learned knowledge of actual high-end manufacturing processes but also the cultural connections that are purely based on emotional perceptions, transforming ordinary objects into status symbols.

The objects we surround ourselves with, besides those serving a purely functional purpose, are a reflection of who we are or who we aspire to become. This added value of objects goes beyond simple

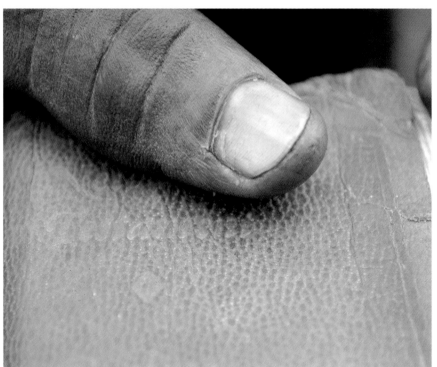

Photo by Rhadika Balla

Joseph is a religious man from Gomboi Village in Ghana. His most prized possession is his New Testament. He bought it used, as it was small enough to fit his pocket. He appreciates the leather cover since it prevents wear and tear, making it easy to carry it around.

functionality and becomes a reflection of our own physical experiences and the emotional connections we make with the world. Added value can be real or it can be just a perception. Either way, the goal of creating aspirational and desirable objects is at the core of CMF design.

(1) Real value will most likely be tangible and measurable through the use of high-end materials, intricate surface finishes or complex manufacturing processes, utilized to provide a product with better quality, higher performance and therefore, a higher price point.

(2) Perceived value on the other hand, can be created in order to provide a product with the appearance of being high-end. This can be achieved through the use of low-cost novelty surface finishes, eye-catching colour combinations, or by creating an overall aesthetic composition with the resemblance to a luxurious object. It is possible to convey a sense of prestige at an affordable price, without necessarily using expensive materials or technologies.

CULTURE

Understanding the cultural background of the targeted consumers and engaging with the context in which the product will be placed, are fundamental steps for a successful product and brand positioning. Aesthetic perceptions change based on cultural backgrounds. There are different and ever-changing influences for each consumer group. Even consumer groups are constantly shifting, merging and evolving. Products need to support different aesthetic values and aspirations according to different influences or trends, which can be local, global or a fusion of both.

Since aesthetic preferences are directly linked to different CMF elements, the same colour, material or finish can be perceived differently depending on culture. For example, novelty and new access to prestigious brands and iconic products are the main aspirations for the growing emerging middle class in countries such as Brazil and China. Although these two cultures are very different from each other, novelty is a common, coveted attribute for products and experiences, as it is considered a symbol of progress, optimism, social mobility and self-improvement. In Western Europe on the other hand, with the increasing economic hardship of recent years, austerity, knowledge and experiences are becoming the main aspirations of consumers, reflecting a spiritual and moral enlightenment. These values are brought to products through the use of authentic or sustainable materials, such as wood and metals, which tend to age gracefully with time, developing rustic and pleasant patinas.

It is very likely that emerging middle class consumers from young

Nespresso and the Chinese lifestyle brand Shanghai Tang collaborated on a four-item collection in 2012, the year of the dragon, featuring the mystical and majestic dragon as a key design element. The collection takes the coffee connoisseur on a complete multi-sensory journey while localizing Nespresso brand and globalizing the Shanghai Tang brand.

economies would not settle for products offering rustic and aged looks as they would not fulfil the physical representation of their aspirations. In the same way, polished, reflective and vibrant colours and surfaces would most likely be perceived a symbol of loud "bling" or "new money" by most Western European consumers, for whom, a more quiet aesthetic is preferred.

EVOCATIVE NATURE

Materials and finishes have an evocative nature. Every person has a pre-conceived idea about a certain material's functional and perceived value. This is key because in many cases, the evocative meaning of a material or colour can be far more powerful the actual one. Traditionally, the materials that better seem to maintain their real and perceived value through time, from culture to culture, are those derived from natural resources. Minerals like diamonds, crystal, glass and precious metals such as gold, platinum and titanium are at the top of the list when it comes to high real and perceived value. In fact, a number of contemporary finishes try to emulate visual characteristics of original precious minerals and metals in order to evoke a feeling of high end. Other materials have a lower perceived value. Plastics, for example, have a more disposable nature, which recently has been connected with environmental issues. Another aspect that aids the low perceived value of plastic is its ease of manufacturing which allows for the production of high volumes at a relatively low cost, making it an ubiquitous material. Despite of being a highly functional material, its lack of rareness – especially in recent times – is pushing it towards the low end side of the perceived value spectrum.

Transparent table by Nendo with a moulded wooden-like surface texture. By moulding a natural wood grain into the plastic, an evocative visual and tactile reference is created, making a new product appear more familiar and elevating its perceived value.

Recently a new paradox between materials' functional properties and their visual appearance has emerged, generating contradiction and debate between how a material looks and what functional properties it is able to offer. Smart materials no longer need to be rigid or voluminous in order to have the strongest resistance to impact. Re-engineered polycarbonate, for example, is currently utilized to make sunroof panels for high-end sports cars, not only because of its high resistance to shock properties but also because of its light weight.

VISUAL DESIGN LANGUAGES

Visual design languages are the overall composition of forms, lines, materials and in general visual cues of products. They reveal the point in time when objects were created and the available technologies that shaped them. Sometimes these elements become iconic representations of not only function but technology and time.

The physical appearance of contemporary products is not always a reflection of their targeted functionality but in many cases becomes an emotional trigger charged with a powerful aesthetic expression. By sending visual messages about key functionalities of the product or by enhancing more intangible elements linked to aspirational lifestyles, CMF design plays a powerful part in creating iconic and instantly recognizable visual languages.

Visual languages are of vital importance when positioning products on a specific market tier or a consumer segment. Some visual languages are rooted in historical references that have become iconic with the passing of time. Other visual languages in turn, are a consequence of technical material innovation and performance, which has radically changed manufacturing processes, form factors or functionality. A good example is the use of carbon fibre in consumer products today. Carbon fibre has functional properties of strength, durability and weightlessness to the point, that in many cases a surface making reference to carbon fibre, can help a product to convey the message – real or perceived – of being light-weight and high-performing.

One interesting example of iconic aesthetics is our constant desire to re-visit the past by looking back to previous decades. Our contemporary reference to vintage is deeply charged with images of affection and memorabilia of a recent past, generally influenced by the non-digital era. Such is the case of traditional Polaroid photography, hand-written calligraphy or the resurgence of the "makers". In an increasingly digital world, products offering an emotional connection with these attributes are becoming highly coveted by consumers.

The Polaroid SX-70 Land Camera designed by
Henry Dreyfuss in 1972, represents an iconic
visual design language revolving around clear
functional elements. A collapsible SLR is
highlighted by the practicality of a polysulfone
plastic frame with a copper-nickel-chromium
alloy layer and the use of leather for the outer
grip areas. Today the iconic image of a Polaroid
camera is utilized as a graphic element to denote
picture-taking functionality. Product courtesy
of Amaya Gutierrez.

FUNCTIONAL CONTEXT

In the practice of colour, material and finish design, context is everything. Understanding and leveraging the right context where products will live can make the difference between a successful or a failed product.

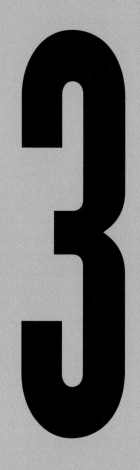

TARGET CONSUMERS

There are different functional needs and expectations when it comes to interacting with a product. Clearly defining and identifying the consumer group will help to design and target products more accurately. Target consumers are the outcome of a process commonly known as consumer segmentation. In order to target them more accurately with customized messages or products, large and small companies classify people into groups according to a set of similar characteristics and consumption behaviours. Depending on the business model, companies may target only one or several consumer groups.

To create well-targeted CMF design, it is very important to work closely with the people who create the consumer segmentation. Within large organizations, they can be part of an internal division which is usually called "consumer insights". They can also be external agencies fully dedicated to consumer understanding. Once the consumer segments have been clearly defined; it is the job of the designer to bring them to life by materializing their aspirations into tangible design elements. Normally this work is done by professionals who have experience and backgrounds like design insights or design ethnography and are able to bridge the gap between the world of consumer insights and the world or design. These are key people to work with in order to ensure that new products are well received by the right group of consumers.

As part of the product development process, companies often schedule several rounds of consumer feedback with a series of focus groups in which potential product users are invited to view a set of physical prompts or appearance models that are close enough to the final product, both aesthetically and functionally, in order to provide real-time feedback. Although this practice is controversial for some – who state that consumers cannot anticipate the future – it can help anticipate potential preferences in terms of aesthetic wants and needs or in terms of functional challenges that may arise throughout the product usage.

PHYSICAL ENVIRONMENT

The functional context in which products will be utilized influences a great number of decisions regarding its colour, material and finish specifications. There are different types of physical environments to consider when specifying colours and materials. One of them is the space where products will be fully functional and operational. This can be an interior or an exterior or a combination of both, depending on the product.

Sports equipment for example, will necessarily have to comply and fulfil a number of technical specifications related to the performance of such sport. If the sport happens outdoors, the CMF design must consider different aspects connected to environmental conditions, such as extreme exposure to sunlight or humidity resistance.

There is also the personal environment, which is tightly connected to the personal space and the lifestyle of the user. Objects do not live in isolation but coexist in the same space with other products and in different arrangements, depending on the user's aesthetic preferences, values and aspirations. These considerations are particularly important because they help us think in terms of overall lifestyle and systems of products, interconnected functionally or aesthetically, rather than single

Photo by Kevin Bethune

Skate boarder in training with his corresponding sports gear and lifestyle accessories which are not only unique in terms of materials, but also in terms of aesthetic lifestyle. Venice, California.

31

or isolated items. Projecting an entire product range or brand to be part of an entire eco system of products will ensure quicker and better adoption from the users.

PRODUCT CATEGORIES

Within different industries, there are different families of objects sharing similar functionality or brand strategy, targeting a specific group of users, or presenting a common formal and visual aesthetic. There can be several classifying principles for product categories and sub-categories, most of which are a combination of all these characteristics. Product categories are of crucial importance because they ensure the correct market positioning of goods and therefore a higher potential to reach the right audience via different channels, such as marketing, advertising, retail environment, e-commerce and other "touch points". Regardless of the type of product the CMF is designed for, it is necessary to ensure a thorough understanding of the product category it belongs to, in order to correctly specify both its functional and emotional design attributes.

Photo courtesy of Bell & Ross

Bell & Ross product categories are differentiated by clear design and CMF elements. The left watch, the BR 123 Original Carbon, is part of the Vintage Original collection and the right one, the BR-X1, belongs to the Aviation collection

**Cyclist in motion showcasing his own
professional bicycle equipment in use.**

Photo by Dice Yamaguchi

Bell & Ross is a brand that creates and markets its collections based on product categories with clear design elements that have become iconic through time. The Vintage Original collection for example is inspired by watches worn by pilots in the 1940's with important differentiating design and CMF elements including the circular shape, the matte finish of the case, the round domed crystal and the finish of the straps – all of which contribute to the feeling of authenticity of timepieces of the past. The Chronograph collection on the other hand offers a sporty design, with an iconic square shape directly inspired by aeronautical flight instruments, providing a contemporary feeling driven by utility.

Other interesting examples of product category positioning are found in the bicycle industry. Although most bicycles have similar functionality, they can be used for a number of different activities, ranging from competitive racing to urban commuting. For competitive racing alone, there can be different sub-categories including cycle-cross, mountain bike, track cycling and BMX. Urban commuting bicycles on the other hand, will be targeting short-distance, casual riders who are highly driven by urban lifestyle, and therefore this category of bicycles will be more style oriented with less functional features.

TIME TO MARKET

Based on technical constrains, external regulations and required product performance, there are different life cycles in every industry, making some products harder to produce and longer lasting than others. CMF design must carefully consider the useful life cycle of products in order to guarantee its accurate performance and enduring aesthetic appeal.

Not all CMF design approaches are suitable for all industries. While certain materials, colours or surfaces may look good on a range of products, they may not transfer well onto other applications. Variable aspects to design such as product dimensions, scale and ultimately, the end purpose of the product itself, are important considerations when translating a CMF design approach from one industry to the next. This has to do with the different speeds of aesthetic cycles in different industries and in some of them, certain combinations and aesthetics become visually tiring faster than in others.

Different industries rely on different product and time-to-market cycles. Consumers already have certain expectations from products in terms of functionality and aesthetics according to the category they belong to – apparel, consumer electronics, automotive, etc. – and these expectations should always be anticipated and managed.

In general, consumer goods that are created through longer time-to-market cycles also tend to stay in the market for longer periods of time. Depending on the industry, consumers will more likely invest higher quantities of money in products that are longer lasting then in products that have a shorter lifespan and fade away with seasons.

Fast-pace industries allow for bolder aesthetic experimentation when it comes to CMF design, while slow-paced industries rely on more traditional and long-lasting aesthetic attributes. They focus on the creation of timeless or more classic aesthetics, which will preserve their real and perceived value for a longer period of time.

In fashion for example, the lifespan of goods is defined by seasons.

Market cycle graph showing different product industries and their market cycles.

This sets up a very fast pace for the industry, where collections are typically designed looking at 6 to 12 months out. The quality of garments in terms of colours, materials and finishes is therefore not expected to perform or outlast a cycle of about 12 months.

In the automotive industry on the other hand, companies are looking at longer development times due to a slower pace of adoption and implementation of new technologies. Cars are typically designed looking 3 to 5 years out. This implies a longer lasting approach to colours, materials and finishes which is tightly connected to the development and adoption of new technologies.

The ideal CMF design offering will ensure longevity and timelessness of aesthetic and functional elements for products created with a longer life cycle in mind, and quick personalization opportunities for what is considered a fast "product update" supported by changing or tweaking small portions or coloured parts within the same line of products.

MARKETPLACE

In many cases, the marketplace itself dictates the product innovation cycle. Market retailers drive an important aspect of the creation of CMF design variants, as they directly request exclusive colours, materials or finishes from product manufacturers. This strategy helps them to differentiate themselves from the competition while bringing a sense of exclusivity to consumers within mass-market products. Such is the case of mobile device retailers in the United States where different carriers request at least one exclusive colour to generally match their brand colour. Through this approach, the products offered by different retailers can be exactly the same in terms of form and functionality, but each will have unique exclusive colours.

In the context of retail, different product categories are called SKUs (stock-keeping units). These are unique identifiers for each distinct product or CMF design variant that can be purchased. Depending on the variations in colours, surface patterns or materials made to one product; the number of SKUs will also increase. Managing inventory then becomes an important part of CMF product placement within the marketplace. There are certain items that move faster than others. Sometimes, even after extensive trend tracking and forecasting, some products simply won't sell needing therefore to be modified or removed from the shelves quickly. In order to produce a successful retail-driven portfolio of products from a CMF design perspective, it is crucial to work tightly with the marketing the end point of sales teams.

CMF CREATION

CMF design should be conducted in parallel with product ideation and development so that it can support and enhance physical aspects such as scale, form and functionality.

STEP I **INFORMATION GATHERING**

There are many different pieces to the puzzle of CMF design. Getting all these pieces together will help maximize time and results. The first step consists of gathering as much information as possible about the product to be designed.

One approach to gathering information is to visit consumers who are already using the products and interview them by formulating questions focused on functional features related to colours, materials and finishes. This process can help draw interesting insights related to functional elements, which may not be fulfilling consumers' functional or aesthetic needs. A very effective way to approach this research is by asking users to empty their wallets, their pockets or in specific product cases, their backpacks, while describing each of the objects they have and its corresponding functional and/or aesthetic benefit. This will give us an idea of the different objects that surround the user and the context where the product will have a useful life.

Product Brief

The product brief is a short summary document outlining the overall scope of the project, the specific task at hand, the budget and the expected timeline. It is the single most important piece of information required in order to initiate the CMF design process. Moreover, the better the quality of a product brief, the clearer the task and the more successful the design. Ideally, a good product brief includes as much information as possible about the target consumers such as age group, gender, geographical location, type of market and product category (exclusive, mainstream or low-end). Also any market research and competitors information, such as products that are already out there with potentially interesting and competitive features worth considering, is very useful.

For independent consultancies, the product brief comes directly from the client. Within large organizations that have embedded CMF teams, it may come from the product planning, the marketing department or it can be created in conjunction with the overall product design team. In any case and for best practices, it is never recommended to initiate any work without receiving it and understanding the requested product brief.

Since CMF design is directly related to manufacturing costs, once the product brief is received, it is crucial to understand and establish the possible accomplishments in terms of manufacturing technologies within the given time frame and budget. This process involves managing the expectations of the client in terms of actual budget and desired task. As a general rule, creating completely new CMF designs will automatically

Photo and backpack contents by cyclist Dice Yamaguchi

One way to gather information about a product is to ask consumers who already use it to empty their backpack and describe the contents' benefits.

increase the project complexity and will most likely result in higher manufacturing costs as well as longer production and time to market.

There can be different levels of CMF design involvement required. The most basic level of involvement normally consist of supporting the "refresh" of the existing product portfolio. This can be achieved by creating new colours, materials or finishes variants without necessarily changing the existing product design. In these cases, there is no need to develop new parts or new form factors, instead the focus is on creating a refresh based on emerging aesthetic and consumer trends. Some examples of a basic level project could be changing the colour of a bottle cap from blue to green in order to make it look more sustainable or tweaking the graphics of a product label into a hand-written font, in order to make it feel more authentic. Both of these examples belong to what is known as the FMCG industry (fast moving consumer goods), where fast product turnaround is expected while operating under very tight budgets.

The most complex level of involvement consists of specifying many different new parts and components for a single product. Such is the case in projects involving the CMF design for aviation and automotive interiors, where besides the many different parts – a car interior typically has more than 350 parts – there are also many different materials, finishes and technical requirements for every part according to industry standards. Product innovation cycles in these industries tend to take longer to be achieved. The CMF design process for automotive interiors typically begins about 42 months before initiating its production.

Surveying the Market

Surveying and analysing the market before starting to create the CMF design is a fundamental grounding exercise to get closer to the target consumer. Competitors' analysis and market research are complex processes, generally conducted by experts with professional backgrounds in marketing, statistics, and business strategy. This work consists of mapping or positioning existing and future products according to market tiers and target consumers. Within large organizations, this information is generally available through the consumer insights or portfolio planning departments. Within smaller companies, this process is normally outsourced to external consultants. It is a good professional practice to request and to be informed of any available or existing competitor's analysis data.

For CMF design purposes, the process of surveying the market is conducted by designers and utilized specifically to draw design insights. This process can be conducted through different methodologies involving design ethnography or design thinking, for which there are plenty of existing sources, bibliographies and references. Key is that the market survey processes conducted by designers will by nature focus more on qualitative, rather than quantitative methods of assessment.

One approach is to visit the market place to observe, photograph and purchase similar products or potential competing products. This process gives an idea of existing functional features and aesthetic trends currently happening in the marketplace. Normally there is already a lot of innovation out there worth to be noted and in some cases improved – an approach that can avoid wasting time and resources trying to re-invent the wheel.

Visiting and surveying the market can also involve cross-pollinating ideas from different industries and anticipating similarities of product preferences and usage. For instance, home appliances and consumer electronics are currently merging into an entirely new product category where functionalities such as touch screens or motion sensors, which were previously exclusive to consumer electronics, have entered the home arena.

STEP 2 ESTABLISHING A NARRATIVE

Besides the technical and practical work that lies beneath CMF design, it is equally important to create and develop an engaging narrative for every project.

Storytelling

Storytelling is a compelling way to communicate the design in order to engage clients and ultimate consumers, through key visual elements and concrete messages. This process is more effective if it is grounded on real world events, emerging consumer behaviour or current market trends, so that it will not only make the story more relatable but also more relevant and engaging. There are different ways to build a story but most of them initiate by creating a general context or a framework and then connecting the initial problem or challenge with the proposed design strategy in a cohesive way.

Storytelling is in itself an entire discipline, but key for CMF design is that the message of the story, besides being relevant to actual market events, also has to be intriguing, creative and unique from a colour, material or technology perspective. If we take Nike for instance, their stories are often rooted in material and technology innovations, which are so disruptive and innovative that they become also part of the marketing message. Nike Flyknit for instance, promotes the fact that the shoes are created with an ultra-strong yard knit woven into different textures, shaping the form and eliminating unnecessary weight.

Not all stories are right for all products however, even if they are

A collection of different images, objects, materials, textures and key words, selected to create and communicate an engaging narrative.

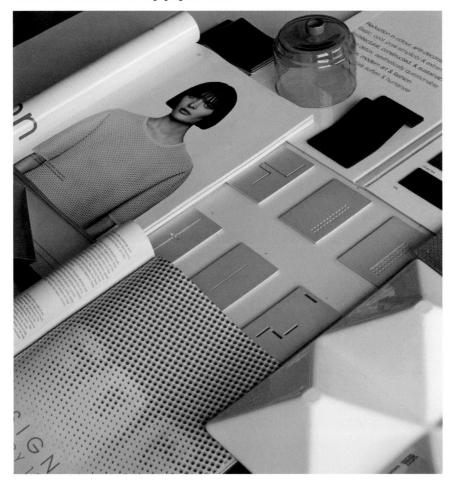

current. It all depends on what is good for the brand, the product and the consumer. In some cases the key story is already part of the brand and thus must be transferred into the different CMF elements – think of Coca-Cola and the happiness campaign, which immediately triggers a specific set of colours and graphic elements in our mind. In other cases it is possible to embed the brand with a new message based on a fresh CMF story. Some key stories that are developing at the moment in a cross-industry approach include, honesty of materials and sustainable manufacturing processes, as well as aspects involving local sourcing, respect for traditional know-how and skill preservation. All of them are rooted in a collective return to consciousness that we are experiencing at the moment, which is pushing us to re-evaluate how products are made, where they came from and what their actual environmental impact is.

The Power of Trend Tracking

During my professional practice, I have developed a substantial and compelling process for understanding and working with trends, from defining what they actually are, to mapping them according to different categories and influences in order to draw different insights. This process happens now naturally on an on-going basis almost like a trained intuition. The main essence when working with trends is to understand that they are not static, but a fast moving, living entity which is always changing, merging and diversifying.

There are different labels of trends, ranging from the macro level, which involves big picture changes and events, to the micro level, which focuses on tangible and quantifiable manifestations of the macro trends. Consumer products and consumer goods respond to a number of shifts in technologies, socio-cultural attitudes and general dynamics of offer and demand within the market place. Understanding, managing and leveraging this context is where the professional field of trend tracking comes in. The trend tracking process is based on constant observation, documentation and analysis of different shifts within the market context. Since this is an ongoing process that runs in parallel with the design of products, it also allows us to look back in time in order to discover patterns of evolution which can in turn, help anticipate possible future scenarios, as well as emerging consumers' needs, desires and aspirations.

When designing colours, materials and finishes, all levels of trends are important. Although some brands tend to connect colours and materials with micro-trends only, it is important to also understand the impact that big picture level trends will have on the products we are designing. One interesting case is how emerging technologies are enabling materials to be thinner, lighter and stronger, and thus driving the use of more translucent, layered and softer colour effects. This trend is based not only on visual aesthetics but also on actual functional benefits provided by new technologies.

When it comes specifically to colour trends, different colours or colour combinations can be driven by many factors including changes within the economic landscape. For instance, in recent years the price of gold has increased in the stock market, spiking demand for the material together with a new wave of gold-like consumer products and a new appreciation for this noble metal. Likewise, the re-birth of natural pigments, which derives from global concern for the protection of the environment and the support to more localised and sustainable production methods, is driving totally new colour design strategies and marketing campaigns.

Several companies, who are also suppliers of paints, coatings and pigments, create colour forecasting books and brochures on a seasonal basis, in order to promote their brand and their most recent colours and surface innovations to their potential clients. In these publications, colour is promoted in parallel to inspirational visual mood boards, statistic colour data and actual physical samples presenting the new effects. The process has been a common practice within the automotive industry for many years, at least since 1987, as traditionally this was the very industry that drove colour trends.

There are companies whose focus is solely to research, create and produce physical and digital trend forecasting tools including books, audio-visual presentations and a series of inspiring prompts to inspire and guide the work on CMF trend forecasting and design. For some of these companies the focus is more fashion and style oriented, while for others it is more about the materials with their corresponding visual and seasonal effects.

Creating Personas

Creating personas is one of the many different types of design ethnography tools, utilized to obtain and communicate cues and insights about consumers. Personas are archetypes or representations of people, their life, desires, aspirations and values. They are based on real data and not on stereotypes or cultural assumptions, in fact, creating personas based on real world data will help us avoid fixating on stereotypical ideas or misconceptions about markets or consumers.

The main difference between personas and mood boards is that personas focus mainly on the lifestyle context – social activities, environments, culture – while mood boards focus on key and concrete aesthetic cues to support the design process. It is recommended to create personas and mood boards in parallel when working with CMF design because, while personas bring our consumer's world to life, mood boards connect consumers directly with specific visual and functional elements of design.

Creating Mood Boards

Mood boards are a conceptual aid created to provide instant inspiration and an emotional connection with the targeted consumers. They represent their desires and aspirations as well as the look and feel of the products and objects within their physical world. Mood boards don't always need to be completely realistic or literal, they can also be a projection or an aspirational lifestyle represented with different visual cues.

Normally, mood boards are utilized within companies as a way to materialize and articulate intangible, aspirational values into visual and functional aesthetic elements. In most cases they work as style guides or look and feel directions for the further creation, development and

Collection of booklets created and distributed
by the trend forecasting and publishing agency
Trend Union, during their seasonal trend briefing
sessions. The books highlight the main topics
presented during the season through the use of
powerful imagery and text.

Set of trend books created and distributed by
Bridge of Weir® a company that specializes in
the production of fine upholstery lathers. The
books showcase the latest surface texture and
colour trends with corresponding samples and
inspiring visuals.

Mood board series "Connected Living" (top) and "The New Normal" (bottom) were created based on emerging macro trends, illustrating the link between macro trends and CMF palettes. They provided inspiration and guidance on how to use the new CMF palettes within BlackBerry® design teams. They were presented as posters and brochures for easy communication. Trend research, story boards and physical mood boards by Janice De Jong, Blackberry® and Studio Liliana Becerra Inc.

implementation of products. They can be digital (image based), physical (object based) or a combination of both digital and physical, as long as the information needed to further create a CMF palette is clearly articulated.

The key to a good mood board for CMF design, is to find or create the right visuals, images or objects needed to define the visual design language, style and other aesthetic elements such as colours, textures, surfaces and materials, in order to support a cohesive message. It is usually very hard to find the right images for a mood board. In fact, in some cases it is a good practice to create and photograph images specifically for it as part of the process – off course if time and budget allow for it.

As a rule of thumb a mood board should loosely include the visualizations of the following elements: the consumer target/persona including hobbies and aspirations, the environments in which the product will live (interior or exterior) and three or more products that are already part of the persona's physical life. The specific content of a mood board will depend on the type of products being designed and the amount of information required in order to convey a clear message, usually less and precise is more.

Regardless of the order of the images and elements, if we are designing the same product for different consumer segments or users, all the mood boards should have exactly the same components and ideally, the same layout so that it is easier to visually compare and differentiate the look and feel for each. Basically, by having the same mood board layout and content for different consumer segments, we will be able to compare "apples to apples" and appreciate the differences and similarities between them.

STEP 3 CREATING A CMF STRATEGY

A CMF strategy carefully considers how users relate to products through a series of touch points: from the first interaction to the long-term usability, and ultimately the product re-purchase.

The CMF Indicator

The CMF indicator is a thinking tool that I created to guide CMF projects through the creation of palettes and their corresponding design strategy. It's recommended to be used at the very beginning of the process when the overall ideation starts. Although there are several existing qualistic tools to position and map out sensorial and functional attributes of products, the CMF indicator presents a simplified way of understanding and leveraging both.

Using the CMF indicator is simple: every sample should go through a qualification process either as a functional or as an emotional element (or as both) in order to understand what is required in terms of effect, functionality and emotionality.

Functional Attributes

The left side of the CMF Indicator comprises the more rational elements and characteristics of design, defined here as the functional attributes. By definition, they tend to have a more permanent nature, represented by tangible, quantifiable measures, as well as by technical and physical performance requirements involving properties such as: durability, rigidity, flexibility and strength.

Durability involves choosing a material or a finish based on how long the product is expected to last and planning how it will age and/or wear off throughout time. Longevity and beautiful ageing are characteristics that make certain materials – like leather or metals – more desirable than others. If on the contrary, a shorter life span is expected of a product, attributes such as easy discarding and recycling are key, prompting the use of easy recycling materials and practical material combination/construction methods.

Although these two are opposite characteristics, they are very related. The more flexible a material or surface, the less rigid it will be. This is important because depending on the required functional properties of a product; materials are expected to have certain level of both.

Flexible materials, such as rubber or elastomers for example, allow for shape recovery after stress has been applied to them and because of this, they tend to be more forgiving when it comes to withstanding dents and scratches. Rigid materials such as glass or brittle plastics on the other hand, are more prone to breakage despite presenting a solid surface.

Both materials' properties – rigidity and flexibility – can be increased or decreased through fabrication processes or through the application finishes such as soft touch for paint or plastic and anti-shatter coatings for glass.

Different materials can withstand different levels of applied forces or efforts. Strength is important, especially for products requiring high-performance resistance against wear and tear, strong sudden impact and other forms of physical pressure. A material's strength is directly related to its expected useful life as most consumer products are expected to break at some point or another.

The traditional visual perception of strength is currently shifting. Visual strength used to be connected with heavy and robust materials, because of their structural resistance to wear and tear. With current developments of material technologies involving super formulations of light carbon composites or materials engineered at a Nano level, struc-

THE C/M/F INDICATOR

Functional Attributes	Emotional Attributes
Permanent Nature	**Flexible Nature**
Quantitative facts	Qualitative facts
Tangible	**Aspirational**
Measurable	**Evocative**
Performance requirements	Aesthetic requirements
Technical	**Trend Influences**
Physical	**Emotive Perceptions**
Keywords	Keywords
Durability	**Contemporary**
Rigidity	**Youthful**
Flexibility	**Luxury**
Strength	**Classic**

HIGHLY FUNCTIONAL   HIGHLY EMOTIONAL

C ————————————————————⬤———
M ———⬤————————————————————
F ———⬤————————————————————

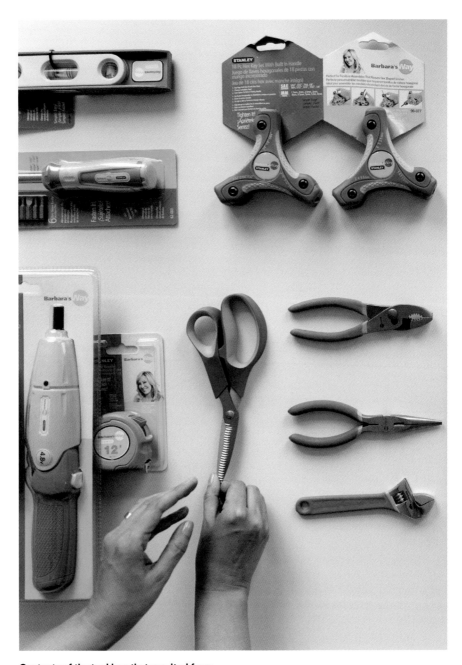

Contents of the tool bag that resulted from the partnership of Barbara's Way's and Stanley Tools. The tools were designed with suitable ergonomics for female body dimensions and a target consumer driven CMF design strategy.

tural surfaces of products are increasingly becoming thinner, lighter and stronger, deceiving preconceived visual aesthetics.

Emotional Attributes

Emotional attributes tend to have a more flexible or changing nature depending on external influences, emotional values and ever-changing market trends. They correspond to qualitative facts involving aspirational and evocative elements. Some of their attributes involve adjectives such as classic, contemporary, active, youthful, luxurious, etc. All these concepts are based on an external perception of how materials present a story and tend to change and evolve over time, depending on many influences.

In most cases, the emotional attributes of products are not achieved only with the selection of one colour, one material or a specific finish effect, but rather through the combination of all of them together with the final product and marketing strategy. Many elements have to converge when it comes to creating highly emotional products, which is why working hand in hand with experts from different disciplines is so important.

Neutral Attributes

Some attributes are neutral because they can be adjusted to be highly functional or highly emotional, depending on product requirements. Among them are tactility and comfort, but there can be more depending on the type of industry and product.

The human ability to touch and feel a material is a fundamental aspect of CMF design. Tactility can enhance the visual appearance of a product and simultaneously support its functionality. In many cases, tactility is an inherent characteristic of a material or a surface – like the softness of cotton and silk. Tactility can also be an "added" property, achieved through different finishing processes, such as sand blasting for glass or pattern stamping for metal.

Because tactility is all about interactivity and responsiveness of a surface to the touch, it is key to specify the right tactility properties expected of a material during the design of a product. For example, if a surface is expected to provide a good grip to the user, its tactility should be rugged and non-slippery. If the goal is to create a warm and comfortable surface, the tactility of the materials should be soft, slightly flexible and inviting to the touch.

Comfort is a required property for most products, but especially those designed to be in close contact with the human body or with the skin. In industries like medical goods, wearable electronics, apparel, automotive and aircraft design, a high level of comfort provided by the materials is expected. Depending on the application however, materials must provide users with high-performance properties as well. Textiles for instance, are utilized in these industries because, beyond providing comfort, they can comply with specific regulations and requirements, such as fire retardancy, water resistance, breathability and acoustic isolation.

STEP 4 UNDERSTANDING PART BREAK UP

In order to optimize the product benefits through performance and usability, designing CMF part break ups should go hand in hand with design for manufacturing. The material selection should be done at the beginning of the product design process and not in isolation.

Ideally, part breakups should go beyond simple aesthetic styling of products, and into value propositions that users can recognize intuitively through universal cues. For example, if a colour and material variation is expected of a part – such as a handle or a grip – it should be designed with this functionality in mind and in a material that offers the possibility for multiple colour and texture variations.

A good example of products with intuitive appeal created through visual and physical part break up are utility tools, since their value resides mostly on their functional performance. They are often brightly coloured so that they stand out from their surroundings – usually construction sites – and their functional parts, such as grip areas, are often emphasized through texture and non-slip materials like rubber or silicone.

Besides the intended product functionality, part break up can also be a driver or a consequence of the manufacturing processes. In fact, this approach is currently growing in product design, bringing an entire range of opportunities and constrains. Especially when thinking of the entire life cycle of a product – design for disassembly – or when maximizing manufacturing processed and design functionality.

Permanent Versus Flexible Elements

Part break up can also be utilized as a way of moving products up or down different market price points and consumer segmentation tiers. When products are created with this purpose in mind, there are certain elements designed to be permanent and certain elements designed to be flexible or upgradable through different CMF variants.

The metal chassis of a mobile device, which is also designed to be visible as an external frame detail, is an example of a permanent element. It will repeat itself in all the products of the same range. The covers or the different protective case colours and other smaller parts, are designed for colour and finish variations allowing for product personalization and for an extended portfolio offering.

Within the flexible elements, some CMF variants will be considered entry level. In most cases these are gender or age neutral colours such as black, grey or silver and low cost materials like plastic, elastomer or silicone. The broad appeal of these elements makes the products easier to mass-produce and therefore, readily available in higher volumes to mainstream consumers, at lower price points.

Other flexible variants are regarded to be more exclusive. This is the case with special or limited CMF editions that could include expensive manufacturing techniques or handcrafted details that are impossible to replicate. The focused appeal of these elements makes products more expensive to manufacture and therefore coveted by premium or luxury consumers.

Some material finishing technologies are specifically created to instantly elevate the value of common materials, such as plating for instance. This process provides surfaces with a thin, reflective, metal-looking coating which can elevate the perception of value without adding much extra weight to the treated surface.

As there are many different functional benefits and challenges to every material finishing technology, the last section of this book, Finish Design, is completely dedicated to them.

The Giro Reverb urban riding helmet was taken apart to visualize its materials and part break up. The light, yet tough, in-mould shell wraps around to the inside of the helmet to resist dents and dings, while a self-adjusting fit system eliminates the need to dial in the fit when wearing a cycling or winter cap. The finishing touch is a simple and removable visor that adds a touch of style without compromising cooling ventilation in changing weather.

**These photos show, from top to bottom,
the first, second and third read visual design
elements of the Audi A8.**

Establishing First, Second and Third Read

To create a compelling strategy for a CMF palette, it is useful to begin by organizing samples according to first, second and third read elements, keeping in mind that these are different in every product and industry.

Sometimes the first read corresponds to the main area or the most visible surface we can identify from a considerable distance. In a car for example, the first read is identified as the exterior colour, the size and the overall shape or silhouette. In CMF driven product innovation, the first read will be the material technology and its finishing effect, especially when it makes a strong and iconic visual statement. Some examples include novelty and unconventional surface finishes of high-end cars, which are either completely matte or completely mirrored and therefore uncommon and special.

In most cases, the second read corresponds to the surfacing elements and functional parts, which are normally integrated to the main form. These are generally medium-sized parts that require a closer look in order to be discovered by the end user after interacting with the product. In consumer products, these could be the operating keys and buttons and the touch and feel of them. Second read elements could also be the finishing, colouring effects or texturing details of the main surfaces. If they are painted for instance, the second read will be the effect of the paint – glossy or matte, metallic flake or pearlescent effect, etc.

Usually, the third read corresponds to specific details of the product including borders, trims and accents, which are there to emphasize the functionality or form or simply to elevate the perceived value of the product. These details are of particular importance for high-end and premium products as they represent the extra time and level of craftsmanship invested in it. Some examples of third read elements are stitched, perforated or piping details of car seats or etched perforations on metal surfaces designed to provide illumination, enhance sound or to improve the grip in consumer electronic devices. Sometimes in entry product categories, normally the lowest product tier, third read elements are skipped in order to achieve lower production costs. A high-end auto interior for instance, will have as third read elements the hand-embroidered logo in each of the leather seats. A low-end car interior on the other hand will most likely use a synthetic material like polyurethane instead of leather, with a factory-printed logo on the seats.

Personalized details and third read elements can provide what is called the "added value" of a product. There is a large after market industry focused on personalizing and upgrading products based on CMF details, such as golden brand logos of cars or handcrafted inscriptions for watches and other small accessories. Tom Davis eyewear for instance, offers bespoke eyewear solutions by letting clients select their own CMF design elements and by adding a hand-made inscription with their name in the frame.

Logs are created from newspapers and then cut, resulting in layers of a material resembling actual wood. NewspaperWood forms the basis of several products including the handmade jewellery Sample Series, developed by rENs together with Vij5. The details of the pattern are carefully balanced within the circular space of the pendants.

Scale and Proportion

In terms of surface decoration, the scale and distribution of the patterns, textures and overall composition must be proportionate to the size of the object. An oversized pattern over a small object will make it look unresolved and will therefore lower its perceived and real value. The more intricate the surface detailing and part break up differentiation is, the higher the perceived and real value of a product. In the watch and fine jewellery industry, a handcrafted approach to manufacturing with extreme attention to detail elevates the rarity and exclusivity of the products. This does not necessarily mean that small surfaces should be crowded with decoration but rather that the composition of the different elements involving colours, materials and textures should be well thought out in order to make the product look good as a whole, as well as in its specific details.

STEP 5 CREATING CMF PALETTES

A CMF palette is the physical collection of samples or tangible representations of colour, material and finish corresponding the each of the product parts. Depending on the level of complexity of the product, palettes can vary in size and overall level of detail and complexity. Designing CMF palettes is a process that goes beyond simply picking colour and material samples though. It must be supported by a cohesive and applicable design strategy.

Detail of a CMF palette targeting a collection of airplane seat covers, showcasing different materials with their corresponding samples and numbered specifications. Project by Studio Liliana Becerra Inc. for Zodiac Aerospace.

A good palette should include and carefully present all the necessary information to clearly communicate and articulate the new design proposals. In most cases, CMF palettes are a combination of a digital document and a physical display. Key essential elements are the mood board/persona combination, keywords describing the sensorial and functional CMF attributes, physical samples and the digital or physical visualizations of the proposed designs with their corresponding part break up callouts properly numbered and clearly listed.

Establishing Keywords

The process of creating a successful palette begins by generating a series of keywords or verbal attributes to support the product narrative and its functional characteristics. Normally for every CMF variant that is proposed, a separate palette is required. The keywords can be organized by using the CMF indicator, from the functional to the sensorial side of the spectrum. It is recommended to use actual dictionaries in order to select the right verbal attributes needed to communicate and further guide the process. Linguistics and CMF design support one another. It is important however to keep in mind that meanings and associations of descriptive words and visual elements can vary from culture to culture and from product to product and that each industry has its own technical terminology or jargon when it comes to CMF attributes.

Defining the Part Break Up

The next step is to analyse the part break up of the product (see part break up section) in order to see how many actual parts there are and how many different colours, materials or finishes need to be specified. Since this can be a complex process, it helps to number each of the parts to be specified and to organize them either under permanent/fixed elements or under first, second or third read. It often helps to request an expanded view with all the external parts from the industrial designers or the product engineers as well as orthographic views of the products (front, back, sides, top and bottom), in order to begin the CMF exploration.

Ideally, each of the parts that will change colour or material should be isolated in a separate digital layer. Design programs like KeyShot can render parts of a product in different layers which can later be opened in Adobe Photoshop to be visualized and worked on individually. In terms of computer programs specifically for visualizing colour, material and finish in a realistic way, RTT's Deltagen and Autodesk's Showcase software programs are also good choices.

Inspirational Samples Versus Standardized Guidelines

Following the keywords and the established part break up, the next step of the process is to start gathering samples of colours, materials and finishes. When creating an initial and more inspirational palette, the samples can come from any source. They can be actual objects, existing material explorations, intriguing surfaces, novelty colours or material effects, interesting surface treatments, etc. However, as the palette becomes more grounded on tangible manufacturing technologies, there are standardized guidelines and references to use and follow.

Within large organizations, in order to shorten and maximize production time, it is recommended to obtain and utilize samples from current suppliers, already pre-approved for mass production. For this purposes, companies with internal CMF design teams build and populate their own internal materials library on a constant basis, cataloguing both inspirational and manufactured CMF samples, to be referenced quickly and accurately, depending on project needs. In most cases, every material sample is connected to a supplier.

Existing standardized references systems include Pantone® and NCS® (Natural Colour System) for colours, Mold-Tech plates for plastic textures and the German VDI (Verein Deutscher Ingenieure) scale for surface texture determination, amongst many others. Every material and finish industry has their own guidelines and standards. It is crucial to work hand in hand with the suppliers when ideating a CMF Palette in order to get a sense of what is possible to achieve within the given project brief and the most immediate manufacturing constrains

Mold-Tech surface texture guidelines for plastic surfaces and Pantone books with colour chips for printing and paint.

Photo courtesy of Allsteel Inc.

Clarity Chair digital visualization. The colour bars – not part of the digital configurator – are a useful CMF design tool when it comes to visualizing potential combinations of the different CMF components.

Physical visualization study of colour, material and texture compositions targeting small consumer electronics. Although the form remains constant, the material varies, creating differentiation and exploring different material pairings. Project by Liliana Becerra for Nokia.

Product Visualizations and CMF Harmonies

The process of visualizing different palette options goes hand in hand with the creation of CMF harmonies. These are defined as horizontal or vertical composition bars representing the overall distribution and combination proportion of colours, materials and/or finish, according to the product part break up. The CMF break up of the harmonies should correspond directly with the first, second and third read or the fixed and permanent elements of the products. It is important to visualize different harmonies within the product itself before committing to a final design, as physical material and colour samples might look good together over a work bench, but completely different when applied to the product itself, in different compositions and distributions. It is never recommended to decide on a colour or material combination without first visualizing it either digitally or physically, on the product.

Product visualizations can also be physical "appearance models" or prototypes. Although there are currently very good computer programs capable to create very accurate and realistic tri-dimensional product visualization with corresponding colour and materials variants, creating physical prototypes is highly recommended, especially when products have complex forms and detailed part break ups. They will give a more realistic sense of scale, composition, look and feel.

The physical prototypes do not need to be completely accurate in terms of detail level as long as they are able to gather and communicate the overall form gesture and look and feel of the design. The materials utilized for the physical models can either be the actual final materials or a simulation that gives a close indication of the final product aesthetics. The process of digitally visualizing products before committing to a final design, has also become a point of sale tool for companies that offer mass-customization of their products on line, by offering the possibility of mixing and matching different colours, materials and finishes. The different designs of the Clarity Chair by Allsteel were created through the Clarity Configurator digital tool available on their website.

STEP 6 CMF/ DEVELOPMENT

CMF Development brings together ideation and execution of design concepts through the application of different material technologies. The development phase is where the real possibilities of design and innovation are tested, approved and finally included into new mass production runs.

Creating Technical CMF Specifications

Once the CMF palettes have been decided upon, the process of development begins by identifying which suppliers will be developing pre-production samples according to the new designs. The amount of samples to be developed depends on the complexity of the proposed CMF design elements. As a general rule the higher the number of colours, materials or finishes to be developed, the higher the number of vendors and suppliers that will be involved. Suppliers of different materials and technologies tend to work separately yet simultaneously and in order to properly manage this process, it is recommended to create an accurate and clear technical specifications document for each supplier.

A CMF spec (short for specification) is the most commonly utilized visual and written technical specification document created by designers to guide suppliers through the development of the task at hand. The CMF spec normally consists on an exploded view of the product's elements – created in CAD – with the corresponding callouts and numbers per part. The most commonly and easy to use type of visualization is an orthographic view – a two-dimensional drawing describing a three-dimensional object – presenting in one single page the front, back, top, bottom and the sides views of the product. The more specific the information in the CMF spec is, the clearer it will be for the manufacturer to understand and execute the task.

Each of the call outs should include the name and number of the part, the description of the type of development needed for it and the target sample, which is the visual and tactile reference to be matched. It is always recommended to include a target sample with the supplier's spec and to keep a duplicate sample as a reference to check back on the results once the development is done.

Some of the descriptions of the development needed for the different parts can include aspects such as the type of material (resin, wood veneer, metal, etc.), the gloss level (satin, mate, glossy), the type of finish (brushed, sandblasted, polished for metal), and so on. CMF specs tend to be complex documents that take time to be created and require a lot of attention to be prepared. Good managing, planning and organizing skills are definitely a plus at this stage of the process.

Briefing and Working with Suppliers

Once the CMF specs are done, the next step is to brief the suppliers and make sure that the request is realistic, more specifically, that the requested colour or finish effect can in fact be achieved with the specified materials. There will always be adjustments needed in order to accommodate the manufacturing process and a great deal of compromising while working back and forth with suppliers. Usually the first loop of development is not satisfying, and that is normal. Working with suppliers and manufacturers should be seen as a process of trial and error where new opportunities and restrictions are discovered along the way.

In terms of CMF development time frames, it is recommended to calculate for about three loops of sample matching until a satisfactory outcome can be approved for mass production. Product innovation within CMF design truly resides in the accurate allocation of time and resources for R&D, especially when development time and costs are not underestimated or under planned. In general, the more time allocated for CMF Development the more innovative the results will be.

Photo by Dice Yamaguchi

A professional is revising colour and finish samples provided by a paint supplier, based on a target sample request.

Colour Design

FUNCTIONAL ATTRIBUTES OF COLOURS

Besides being a universal language based on perceptions and emotions, colour has important functional attributes that can improve product perception, performance and usability.

COLOUR AFFINITY

There are important external factors that come into play when working with colours, one of them – which is often under estimated – is one's ability to see colour and differentiate tonality nuances.

Working in the area of colour design – either digitally or physically – requires to have good colour affinity. Beyond a well-trained sense of colour composition, professionals working in this area should be aware of their capacity to discriminate colour differences and tonality nuances.

The lack of colour affinity is a common physiological condition known as colour blindness, which affects approximately 10% of men and 1 in 200 women – accounting for approximately 350 million people around the world.

People with colour blindness or in better words, colour vision deficiency, are only able to see a narrower colour spectrum than people with regular vision. There are different kinds of colour blindness – red blindness, blue blindness and green blindness – and different types of tests to find out if you have any type of colour discrimination deficiency.

Colour Arrangement Test
The most commonly used colour blindness tests are based on hue discrimination or arrangement. The D-15 dichotomous test was introduced

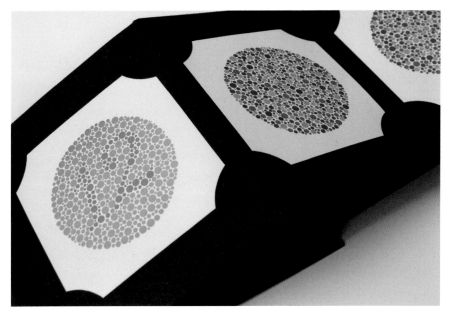

Detail of the Ishihara colour deficiency test.

by Farnsworth in 1947 and was the precursor of modern day colour arrangement tests. The taker of the test has to arrange 15 coloured plates in the correct order. The Farnsworth-Munsell 100 hue test, which has been used by the government and the industry for over 40 years, consists of four trays containing 85 removable colour chips to be arranged in progressive incremental order, spanning the visible spectrum. Colour blind people will arrange several or most colours in the wrong order. Colour discrimination test are also available in digital formats, but factors such as computer settings and ambient light can alter the results.

Ishihara Plates Test

The Ishihara plates test was introduced in Japan by Dr. Shinobu Ishihara in 1917, aiming to evaluate primarily red-green colour blindness. The test consists of 38 different graphs or plates that feature circles made out of coloured dots. Each of them contains a number or a line that is only visible to either individuals with colour vision defect or to those with normal vision. This test is available in printed and digital format.

DARKS AND LIGHTS

Not all shapes and colours go together. Colours can enhance or diminish the form they are applied to. In general colours should be used to make forms stand out in the best possible light.

Darks

When Coco Chanel created the Little Black Dress back in the 1920s, she intended for it to be long-lasting, versatile and accessible to the widest market possible. All of that in a neutral colour. The main feature of black and darker tones in general is that they can make objects appear to be smaller and slimmer than they actually are, while accentuating the overall form or silhouette.

These principles are not only applicable to the human body and to fashion but also to all forms and shapes. When applied to product surfaces, in most cases dark tones create an instantly slimming effect. Utilizing gradation effects from lighter to darker with shades of grey will also help create the illusion of tapering edges or rounding forms.

The downside of surfaces with darker tones is that they reveal dust and scratches more obviously than surfaces with lighter tones. Moreover, if the dark surface has a glossy or highly polished finish, it will reveal oil marks from fingerprints, unless coated with anti-scratch or oleo-phobic finishes.

Lights

Lighter tones tend to reflect back light and therefore bring out little details of a surface including its defects. They have the opposite effect of dark tones; as they reflect more light, they make objects appear to be larger than they really are.

When it comes to dust and scratches however, lighter tones tend to hide them or absorb them better than darker tones. Functionally, white and lighter tones have some positive connotations such as conveying

In products with similar or equal form, it is possible to appreciate the slimming effect of dark colours versus the widening effect of lighter ones.

the feeling of cleanliness and peacefulness. They visually help unclutter surfaces and spaces, making them look more organized.

In typography and graphics, managing the "white space" is quite an important attribute for design, as it actually helps with readability and to convey stronger messages. In interior design, white is connected with modernism and creating white spaces can help to achieve a clean and contemporary environment where other elements can stand out.

QUIET & LOUD

Colour combinations are essential when it comes to triggering different responses in the users and supporting the creation of visual languages. Just as product categories have different market cycles, the same is true for colour combinations.

Neutral tones (Quit)

Neutral tones, including shades of grey and other low-saturated colours, tend to provide a calmer and more classic look, which is also longer lasting. Although neutral tones are also influenced by trends, they don't necessarily fall into fast-paced fads but instead provide a longer and more durable aesthetic. Neutral tones are ideal for products intending to be in use for longer periods of time or for classic timeless objects.

Combinations of neutral tones tend to have a lower contrast than those achieved with brighter or vivid tones. Utilizing lower colour contrast in CMF design allows for the exploration of other surface treatments and construction elements such as textures, trims and other visual effects. In the case of premium products, elements such as tone on tone stitching or tone on tone surface contrast help to convey the perception of exclusivity and high craftsmanship.

Neutral tones with highly refined treatments such as pearlescent or metallic effects are associated with precious metals even when these effects are applied to plastic or other low cost materials. This is why metal plating is considered a very successful finishing technology. It elevates the perceived value of ordinary materials and products through the creation of sophisticated metal-looking surfaces.

When product manufacturers have low budgets to renew their colour offering, or when they simply want the products to appeal to a larger group of users, neutral tones are the preferred choice, as they are ideal when it comes to creating a timeless product portfolio. Interestingly, neutral tones are often preferred by wealthier and more mature markets where consumers are more interested in handing down products from one generation to the next.

Mirror-finished trainers with bright laces contrast beautifully with the grey asphalt.

Photo by Claudia Geidobler

Fluorescents and Brights (Loud)

A combination of vibrant and vivid tones can produce a dynamic and expressive colour composition. Neon-inspired colours and bright tones are normally perceived to be more playful and therefore usually used in younger consumer market segments.

Since brighter colour combinations create a higher level of contrast, they also tend to become more memorable or iconic and therefore have a shorter life span. Since the bright colour cycle moves faster and renews itself more often, these colours are ideal for products that are not intended to be long-lasting, such as product packaging, cosmetics packaging, fast moving consumer goods or after-market accessories for consumer electronics and mobile devices.

Opposite to neutral tones, bright colours are associated with lower cost materials such as plastic, polyurethane, rubber and paint, which are quick and easy to manufacture and to discard. In some cases though, bright tones are utilized by premium or luxury product categories as trim details (the stitching or piping for car seats) or as iconic branding elements for a special products or sports editions.

Functionally, brighter tones are ideal for high performing products, especially for functional sports categories such as cycling, running and mountain climbing, and for utility categories such as home improvement tools, emergency equipment, medical devices, etc. Bright colours allow products to instantly stand out from their surroundings.

COLOUR CONVENTIONS

Colour conventions tend to be universal. From nature to man-made symbols, these conventions are not dependent on seasonal trends. Instead, universal colours are selected to be highly visible and to convey clear informational messages.

Universal Colour Conventions

There are global colour conventions that are purely functional and very important to keep in mind when utilizing colour to denote functionality and designing practical product guidelines and functional parts. These

Photo courtesy of ColorADD, Miguel Neiva

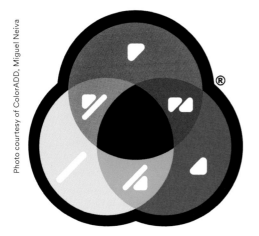

ColorADD enables the colour-blind to identify colours based on five graphic symbols representing the three primary colours, black and white. By relating the symbols, the entire colour pallet can be graphically identified.

Colour Pencils based on ColorADD system.

**ColorADD representation for a
transportation system map.**

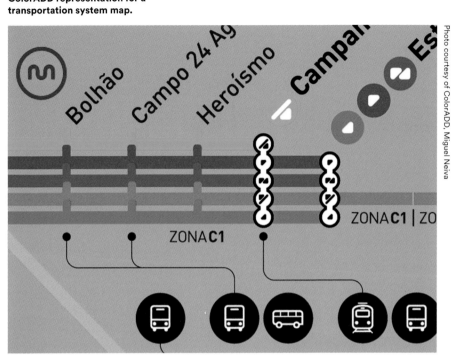

conventions are independent of aesthetics or seasonal colour trends and
tend to be very standardized across cultures and countries.
A green traffic light means 'go', while in red it represents danger and
warns us to stop. In package design, poisonous or potentially harmful
materials are indicated by a black skull warning us of death. Utilitarian
outfits and tools for construction work are often created in bright,
non-complex colours such as green, orange or yellow, so that they stand
out from their surroundings and are easy to identify from a considerable
distance. Depending on the country, road signage is created by applying
different bright colours under a high-tech surface formed by tiny reflective glass beads in order to maximize the reflection and instant recognition of the colour once it is illuminated.

Created Conventions
When creating colour design for functional products such as medical
devices, it is possible to develop new functional conventions. As an example, the insulin colour code chart created by the International Diabetes
Federation, was developed as a universal colour code based on Pantone
references, in order to denote similar preparations of insulin, regardless
of the manufacturer, to be placed on labels in order to avoid confusion in

patients who need to buy insulin from different sources.

Created colour conventions are utilized by different industries such as healthcare, food and beverage, city and urban planning, science, culture and others. A very interesting case of universal colour conventions translated into specific functionality, is the Colour Identification System project ColorADD which translates the three primary colours blue (cyan), yellow and red (magenta) and black and white into five visual symbols. These symbols form the basis of a universal graphic code for people with colour vision deficiency or colour blindness. Through the acquired knowledge of the Colour Addition Theory taught in the early school years, the symbols can be related and the entire colour pallet graphically identified. The system aims to make colour identification and communication more efficient, responsible and inclusive.

BRANDS AND COLOURS

Visual colour branding is an extensive practice involving tangible and intangible elements to create iconic, functional and memorable brand recognition. Colour is an important aspect of branding. It can be so powerful that it can become a large part of the brand equity. While some brands have been recognized for the use of iconic colours, like the Coca-Cola red or the legendary Tiffany's aqua green, other brands seek to convey different emotional messages. In corporate branding, dark blue is used to convey messages of trustworthiness, reliability and seriousness.

Iconic Brand Innovation

An interesting use of colour for brand innovation can be seen when traditional brands with already existing branding colour, launch special edition product series or new technologies designed to enhance the current performance or usability. In this case the original branding elements such as font and colour are preserved and enhanced with a colour accent to signal the new innovation. Some examples include the Porsche e-Hybrid logo, which presents a bright green glow behind the silver letters or, the BMW i8, which uses a bright blue colour to highlight its logo and different areas of the interior trims and accents.

Soft Colour

Besides the visual colour branding for brand logos and corporate identity, which are intended to be perceived as a first read, there are also softer and more subtle brand DNA aspects designed to be perceived slower as the product is being discovered and utilized. Some examples include the

Iconic brand innovation through colour
elements enhancing branding messages about
electrical efficiency in bright green for the
Porsche Cayenne e-Hybrid and bright blue
for the BMW i8.

Sephora and Pantone collaborated for a special edition package of brushes in Tangerine Tango – Pantone 17-1463, colour of the year 2012.

Product courtesy of Amaya Gutierrez's collection

accent colours utilized for the dashboard dials of the MINI Cooper, the orange ambience glow present in all BMW interiors, the red trim accents utilized in Audi interiors and the Mazda red signature exterior colour.

Functional Colour

Functional colour branding can also become iconic based on technical know-how when it has been created to fulfil functional industry needs. The iconic "glow in the dark" utilized in wrist watches, was initially developed as "Luminor". This isotope of tritium-based hydrogen was created for the military and patented by the Italian watchmaker Panerai in 1949, becoming the trade-mark of the brand and later on, a visual colour indicator of the "glow in the dark" functionality.

COLOUR MEASURING TOOLS

The process of colour matching is affected by many different aspects such as the type of pigments utilized, the selected method of application and the base colour or surface texture of the substrate. A range of measuring tools including digital colour readers, light booths and colour correcting lighting can additionally support the process.

Digital Colour Reading

Colour readers are created based on the principle of a colourimeter, which are scientific tools to measure the wavelengths of light. Portable and digital colour readers are utilized to measure and match the colours of various surfaces to a specific colour system, providing different colour conversion values including CMYK and RGB.

New subscription-based business models have recently emerged, revolving around digital colour readers paired with the process of colour collecting, organizing, referencing and sharing supported by mobile apps. Digital colour reading is expected to grow and expand in the areas of product and environmental design, architecture, as well as in the residential and contract paint industry.

NCS (Natural Colour System) Colourpin®, for example, is a digital colour reader that can be connected to a mobile device via Bluethooth® and operated through an app. The pin measures an area with a 12 mm diameter for one second through a measuring principle involving a LED and a 16 grid filtered photo detector array. The app allows users to create digital boards by pinning colours they encounter in different objects, nature or environments. The pinned colours and boards can be saved into a library or further edited and shared with other users.

Colour Matching

Different technologies are used to achieve the same colour on different materials. Therefore, when different parts of a product are required to match one colour sample, it is wise to initiate the process with the part that represents the biggest challenge and then use its final approved sample as a reference for the others. Certain colours and effects are more difficult to achieve than others, depending on the type of material and the nature of the pigment. White for instance, tends to be more translucent or less opaque than other colours. These are important considerations when deciding on the base colour of the substrate material. When applying light-coloured paint over a dark-coloured surface, the combination of those two colours results in a greyer white rather than in a pure white.

Although Pantone colour chips are to be used as target samples, for colour matching there is large consensus between professionals about

The NCS Colourpin®.

the fact that different Pantone chips – even with the same number – might look different due to sun damage or to the length of ownership of the books. Therefore, in many cases, it is better to obtain a target a sample that is created in the exact colour, material and finish effect that is desired.

Light Booths
For colour development and colour matching decision making, there are existing visual colour evaluation systems, normally known as colour matching booths, which offer simulations of different lighting conditions ranging from natural daylight and fluorescent, to ultraviolet. By examining and comparing the developed colour sample with the target sample under different light conditions, it is possible to achieve better and more

accurate colour matches. These booths are created based on international standards for visual evaluation of colour that are used globally across suppliers.

By nature, any colour will look different under varying lighting conditions. The most common types of lights utilized to match different colour samples are natural daylight and fluorescent. As a rule of thumb, when a colour sample held at a 45-degree angle looks very similar to the target sample under these two lights, the colour match can be considered successful and the sample can be approved for production.

COL-OUR exhibition

In 2015, Luca Nichetto produced the COL-OUR exhibition in collaboration with NCS Colour, De La Espada and Triton. The exhibition in Milan showed how the furniture colours were defined for his brand Nichetto. The starting point for the definition of the colour palettes was the Herbarium, an ex-tensive research project by Massimo Gardone on natural elements such as flowers and leaves. Thanks to the NCS Colourpin® and the scientific method of Natural Colour System, Nichetto Studio was able to extract a selection of colours from the Herbarium before dividing them into three tonalities: warm, cold and neutral. Found on every continent and not influenced by a temporary fashion trend, the colour palettes have been applied to ma¬terials and finishes including fabric, wood, stone and lacquer surfaces.

Photo courtesy of Massimo Gardone and Nichetto Studio

Designed by Luca Nichetto and manufactured by De La Espada for the Nichetto brand, the colours of the Stanley Sofa are based on the on the Herbarium project.

CULTURE AND CONTEXT OF COLOURS

Colours are not independent of context. They have a symbiotic relationship with the events and experiences that form the collective memory of the world.

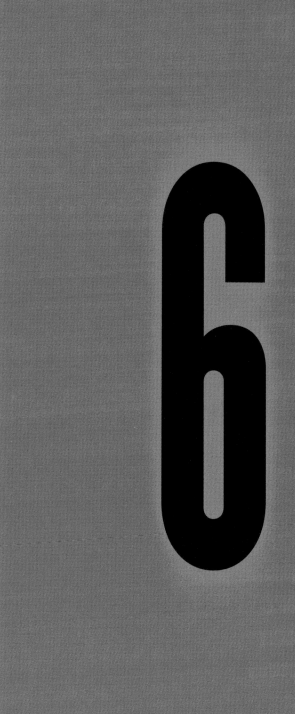

BLACK

Black is a neutral, authoritative colour that can evoke both positive and negative emotions. It can create the feeling of sophistication and emptiness at the same time: it can represent power and dignity as well as pessimism and sadness. In colour psychology, black represents protection from the outside world, and the concealing of emotions. Black is also a classic neutral colour that people often wear to feel slimmer or to fit right in. It is the colour of mourning in the west. The custom of wearing black, non-decorative clothing for days of mourning goes back all the way to the Roman Empire.

Black has mysterious effect on people – some people may feel intimidated by a person wearing black in either formal or casual occasions. It is often associated with seduction and intrigue. It also has a submissive quality to it, like a priest wearing black in order to feel faithful and submissive to God. In Western culture, black is represented as a colour of power, danger, death and rebellion while in Eastern cultures black is seen more as a symbol of wealth, elegance and prosperity.

KEY CULTURAL ASSOCIATIONS OF BLACK

DANGER

DEATH

MYSTERY

CONSERVATIVENESS

ELEGANCE

AUTHORITY

SUBMISSION

POWER

PERILOUS JUICE
Octopus ink

Cephalopods (squids, octopuses and cuttlefish) have ink stored inside an ink sac which they release as an escape mechanism. The dark pigment is released into the water accompanied by a jet of water from the siphon. Its dark colour is caused by its main constituent, melanin. Each species produces slightly differently coloured inks; generally, octopuses produce black ink, squid ink is blue-black and cuttlefish ink is brown. Modern use of cephalopod ink is generally limited to cooking, where it is used as a food colouring and flavouring.

WHITE

White is a crisp, neutral colour that encourages us to think more purely and clearly. It is associated with cleanliness, decluttering and organizing. In colour psychology, it is known as a colour of fresh starts and new creations, acting as a blank canvas. Many people associate the colour white with innocence and youth, recalling a time when they were naive and protected by their families. On the negative side, white can have a cold, isolated feeling, as demonstrated in many medical offices and hospitals.

Since white is a combination of all colours, it is considered an equalizer, often associated with fairness and neutrality. Western cultures perceive white to be representative of purity and peace whereas Eastern cultures believe it represents death, mourning and sadness, especially in China, India and Africa. Even though the colour white may convey feelings of isolation and coldness, it's overall a clean, pure colour that can brighten up a space and make way for the future.

KEY CULTURAL ASSOCIATIONS OF WHITE

PURITY

CLARITY

NEW BEGINNINGS

CREATIVITY

CLEANNESS

INNOCENCE

YOUTH

NEUTRALITY

FILLING GOODNESS
Rice

Rice is the most important food
for a great part of the world's
population, especially in the
warmer climates. China is the
largest producer and consumer.
Rice is usually divided into long-,
medium-, and short-grained.

RED

Red is a vibrant, stimulating colour associated with our basic instincts and senses. While it represents love, passion and beauty in some cultures, it can also represent anger, aggression and war. Red's visual energy promotes a need for action and assertiveness, mainly because it excites our emotions. Physiologically, it activates the body and senses which can result in increased blood pressure and heart rate if largely exposed to it.

Restaurants often use red because of its ability to stimulate one's appetite. While Western cultures see red as a representation of love, warning and anger, Eastern cultures view red as the colour of prosperity, beauty and good fortune, especially China.American cultures perceive blue as a colour of sacrifice and mourning. In general, Western cultures interpret blue as a colour of peace and trust, while Eastern cultures view it as a colour of immortality and virtue.

KEY CULTURAL ASSOCIATIONS OF RED

FERTILITY

SEDUCTION

SEXUALITY

MARRIAGE

ANGER

AGGRESSION

APPETITE

PASSION

LOVE

PIPPIN' HOT ICE
Red chili peppers

Spicy hot, pungent, intense taste fruit from the Capsicum plant originated in the Americas. The substances that give chili peppers their intensity when ingested or applied topically are capsaicin (8-methyl-N-vanillyl-6-nonenamide) and several related chemicals collectively called capsaicinoids. When consumed, capsaicinoids bind with the pain receptors in the mouth and throat responsible for sensing heat. Once activated by the capsaicinoids, these receptors send a message to the brain that the person has consumed something hot. The brain responds to the burning sensation by raising the heart rate, increasing perspiration and releasing endorphins.

ORANGE

Orange is a warm, inviting colour that combines the physical energy of red with the bright happiness of yellow. It represents adventure and risk-taking and like red, it evokes confidence and enthusiasm. This is why most sportsmen and thrill-seekers prefer orange apparel and accessories for their professions and hobbies. Orange is also associated with spontaneity and encourages social communication, interaction, friendship and communities.

Orange has a rejuvenating effect on people as it has a balanced vitality to it. In Eastern cultures, orange is representative of happiness and spirituality, whereas in Western cultures, it represents affordability and optimism. More specifically, orange is often used for safety devices in the United States. The Occupational Safety and Health Administration (OSHA) requires some construction equipment to be manufactured in orange.

KEY CULTURAL ASSOCIATIONS OF ORANGE

ENERGY

ADVENTURE

VITALITY

FRIENDSHIP

WARMTH

CONFIDENCE

CLEVER SNAP
Carrot

Carrot is a vegetable rich in anti-oxidants and minerals. It supports good vision, is a good source of vitamin A and is used to colour food. The carrot gets its characteristic and bright orange colour from β-carotene, and lesser amounts of α-carotene and γ-carotene. A and β-carotenes are partly metabolized into vitamin A in humans. Carrot extracts are used by poultry producers to improve animal skin and alter the colour of egg yolk. Overconsumption of carrots can cause carotenosis, a benign condition in which the skin turns orange.

YELLOW

Yellow is a warm, bright colour that stimulates the mind and encourages communication. It is known psychologically as the happiest colour in the spectrum. It is said that it helps people to focus, aiding with decision-making and with clarity of ideas. Its close relation to the sun makes yellow the best colour for representing enlightenment, happiness and optimism.

Yellow can have a creative effect on some but generates anxiety in others. While being mentally activating, yellow can also unearth a great amount of confidence in someone. Some cultures find yellow to have a negative meaning, like the Greek and the French, whom perceive it to be related to sadness, envy and jealousy, respectively. In general, yellow is perceived to represent happiness, cowardice and caution in the Western culture, whereas it is perceived as sacred and imperial in most Eastern cultures.

KEY CULTURAL ASSOCIATIONS OF YELLOW

VITALITY

FRIENDSHIP

MIND-STIMULATION

CREATIVITY

CONFIDENCE

OPTIMISM

DON'T WORRY, BE CORNY
Corn

Corn, a large grain rich in antioxidants and carotenoids, is a good source of fibre, which provides digestive benefits. Maize is widely cultivated throughout the world. The United States produces 40% of the world's harvest while other top producing countries include China, Brazil, Mexico, Indonesia, India, France and Argentina.

GREEN

Green is a cool, soothing colour that provides emotional and mental balance. It is known to help people relax both mentally and physically, as it is a soothing colour that can help with depression and anxiety. It is an emotionally positive colour that is abundantly present on earth in nature. As a combination of yellow and blue, green provides the mental sharpness of yellow, along with the soothing calmness of blue.

Most Western cultures see green as the colour of luck and nature, while most Eastern cultures see green as a sign of regeneration, hope and fertility. The Japanese culture regards green as the colour of eternal life.

In general, green is a symbol of peace, rejuvenation and harmony, as its abundant presence on Earth balances our mind, body and soul on a daily basis.

KEY CULTURAL ASSOCIATIONS OF GREEN

NOURISHMENT

LUCK

ABUNDANCE

WEALTH

HOPE

PROSPERITY

POSITIVITY

NATURE

LUCKY LICK
Clover

Clover grows freely in abundant crops. It fixes nitrogen and reduces the need for synthetic fertilizers. Clovers occasionally have leaves with four leaflets, instead of the usual three. These four-leaf clovers are considered lucky. Clovers can also have five, six, or more leaves, but these are very rare. The record for most leaves is 56, set on 10 May 2009. This beat the 21-leaf clover, a record set in June 2008 by the same man, who had also held the prior record Guinness World Record of 18.

BLUE

Blue is a cool, calming colour that is connected with trust across cultures as it is perceived as a reliable and responsible colour that exudes confidence and trustworthiness. Most hues of blue evoke a sense of physical and mental relaxation, providing inner peace, tranquillity and calmness. Since blue is a safe colour, it is connected with devotion and religious studies, as well as with authority. In fact, most banks, corporations and brands use the colour blue to evoke a feeling of reassurance and reliability to the customers. On the negative side, blue can also be perceived as predictable, boring and conservative.

Blue has a stress-reducing effect on people mainly because it tends to be orderly and sincere. It is a neutral colour that doesn't like to draw attention, and that may be why it's the most dominant "favourite colour" in the world.

Iran perceives several hues of blue to signify paradise, while Central American cultures perceive blue as a colour of sacrifice and mourning. In general, Western cultures interpret blue as a colour of peace and trust, while Eastern cultures view it as a colour of immortality and virtue.

KEY CULTURAL ASSOCIATIONS OF BLUE

COOL

TRUSTWORTHY

RELIABLE

CORPORATE

CALM

RELAXING

GENERIC

NEUTRAL

KEEP IT COOL
Clitoria Flower

Medicinal, edible plant used to reduce stress, colour food and also as an antidepressant. In traditional Ayurvedic medicine, the Clitoria flower has been used for centuries as memory enhancer, nootropic, antistress, anxiolytic, antidepressant, anticonvulsant, tranquilizing and sedative agent. In Southeast Asia the flowers are used to colour food. In Malay cooking, an aqueous extract is used to colour glutinous rice for kuih ketan (also known as pulut tai tai in Peranakan/Nyonya cooking) and in nonya chang. In Thailand, a syrupy blue drink is made called nam dok anchan, which is sometimes consumed with a drop of lime juice to increase acidity and turn the juice into pink-purple. In Burmese and Thai cuisine the flowers are also dipped in batter and fried.

PURPLE

Purple is a cool, uplifting colour with a sense of spirituality. It can calm the mind and nerves, as well as encourage creativity. From a psychological perspective, purple provides a link between thought and activity, offering a sense of mental balance. As a combination of red and blue, it carries the stimulation of red and the calmness and integrity of blue. Too much purple however, can aggravate depression in some people. Purple's connection to spirituality also makes it related to the imagination and dreams – it is known as an introspective colour that promotes enlightenment. Its close relation and history to royalty and the nobility make purple also a colour of luxury and wealth with regal, extravagant qualities to it.

Western cultures believe purple is a colour of royalty and spirituality, while most Eastern cultures think purple is a colour of sorrow, wealth and mourning. In Iran, purple is a colour of the future, while some Latin American countries perceive it as the colour of death and mourning.

KEY CULTURAL ASSOCIATIONS OF PURPLE

LUXURY

STATUS

ROYALTY

NOBILITY

CHURCH

ROMANCE

SPIRITUALITY

IMAGINATION

BEAT THE BOOST
Beets

A healthy root vegetable rich in antioxidants and nutrients that helps prevent blood diseases. It is rich in magnesium, sodium, potassium, vitamin C, and betaine. Betanin, obtained from the roots, is used industrially as red food colourant, to improve the colour and flavour of tomato paste, sauces, desserts, jams and jellies, ice cream, sweets, breakfast cereals, etc.

SILVER

Silver is a cool, metallic colour that is associated with the moon and the feminine energy. Its illuminative quality implies that silver is a cleansing colour that provides calmness and helps release mental and physical stress. Silver has a reflective effect on people and is believed to draw negative energy out of the body and replace it with positive energy. Its metallic refinement makes it a livelier, sophisticated version of grey, conveying elegant neutrality.

Eastern cultures, like the Japanese and Muslims, perceive silver to represent intelligence and peace, respectively. In the Western world, Native Americans believe silver to be a colour of agreement and truce. In the contemporary world, silver is very versatile; being applied to both high-tech electronics and elegant fashion garments. It is also associated with wealth and prosperity, and more specifically to the professional and corporate arena.

KEY CULTURAL ASSOCIATIONS OF SILVER

HIGH-TECH

REFLECTIVE

SLEEK

MODERN

COOL

FUTURISTIC

WEALTHY

LONG-LASTING

CLASSIC

INTERGALACTIC MIND
Edible silver foil (varaq)

Varaq is any foil layer of very pure metal – typically silver – used for garnishing sweets in South Asian cuisine. The silver is edible, and flavourless. The use of varaq is not considered harmful to the body, since the quantities involved in normal use are minuscule. This however is only true as long as the foil contains only high purity silver.

GOLD

Gold is a warm, metallic colour that represents wealth and prestige in Both Western and Eastern cultures and in almost every country today. Gold relates to masculinity and brings to mind the brightness and energy of the sun, illuminating and radiating energy.

This colour is connected to yellow and brown, becoming a hybrid of brightness and stability. Gold has traditionally been associated with the riches of royalty around the world, what makes it closely related to prosperity.

Although gold has a bright, cheerful quality to it, it can also be perceived as traditional and not as modern as silver. It is connected to all that is successful, triumphant and extravagant.

KEY CULTURAL ASSOCIATIONS OF GOLD

PRESTIGE

LUXURY

TRADITION

PROSPERITY

TRIUMPH

EXTRAVAGANCE

ENERGY

SUN POWER

FLAMBOYANT REWARD
Gold leaf and sugar

Gold leaf is sometimes used to decorate food or drink, typically to promote a perception of luxury and high value. It is usually found in desserts and confectionery including chocolates and mithai. In Asian countries, gold is sometimes used in fruit jelly snacks. It was also used in coffee, particularly during Japanese asset price bubble. In Kanazawa, where Japan's gold leaf production was centered, gold leaf shops and workshops sold green tea and hard candy with gold leaf inside.

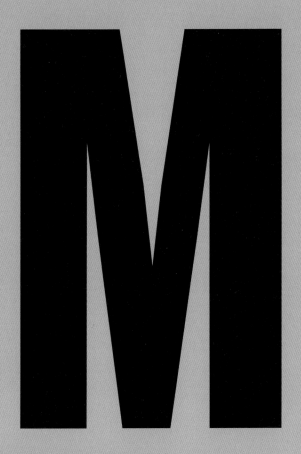

Material Design

MATERIALS FIRST

Designing products around the materials can lead to very creative and often unexpected aesthetic and functional solutions.

MATERIAL COMBINATION STRATEGIES

There are different approaches when it comes to establishing and creating CMF combination strategies. Most of them obey to general principles of aesthetic and visual composition, while others are a result of the materials design approach.

Pairing Materials

Besides specifying every single colour, material or finish as a separate element, it is important to foresee how they will behave when assembled together. Natural materials will want to expand and contract under different environmental conditions such as humidity, heat or external elements. Synthetic or man-made materials on the other hand, don't necessarily absorb humidity or allow water to penetrate and modify its structure. Ideally, materials that go together should have similar physical properties. When materials with different properties are assembled together, the industrial design of the product could allow for the creation of gaps and higher tolerances between materials and surfaces as a functional and visual design element, in order to allow the two materials to expand or contract independently.

A material pairing study explores the aesthetic and functional potential of intersections between plastic and metal. Project by Liliana Becerra for Nokia.

**The backbone of the Ago table, designed by
Alfredo Häberli for Alias, is clearly visible
through the glass top.**

Photo by Studio Phototecnica, courtesy of Alias

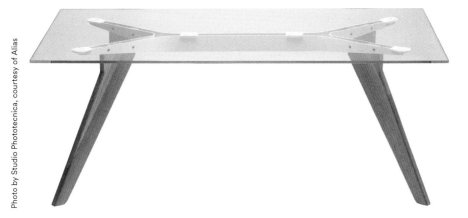

Design for Disassembly

A great emphasis on material combination strategies has surged in recent years for products designed to be "considerate" throughout their entire life cycle by involving a strategy called "design for disassembly". This emerging key area for product and CMF design implies specifying the different product parts and materials to be easily assembled and disassembled for repair, refurbishing or recycling.

One of the greatest paradoxes of our times is that there are products created to have a very short life span, yet manufactured with material technologies that make them hard to recycle at the end of their useful life. A good example of this paradox is a disposable toothbrush whose different parts have been fused together through a co-moulding process. Once different materials – like rubber and plastic in this case – have been fused together, they behave as one single material with different properties: while the soft rubber provides the handle with a good grip, the plastic provides the necessary rigidity to perform the brushing function. The challenge arises when the bristles are worn out before the handle is, and it is not possible to remove them and replace them as a single part. Moreover, during the disposal process, recycling is ruled out due to the contamination of the material stream with foreign particles.

One way for commingled products to have a second life is to grind them up and use them as filler in asphalt and plastic timber. This process is known as "down cycling" and is based on using a material only for its filler and mass qualities and not for its inherent performance characteristics.

There are several aesthetic and functional strategies utilized to create products with disassembling in mind. Some of them involve the use of

**Based on the philosophy "design of reduction",
the Clarity chair preserves only the essential
elements of form and function. A simplified
set of parts can be mechanically disassembled
allowing clear part separation between plastic
and aluminium components.**

Photo by Scott McDonald, courtesy of Allsteel

connectors that snap together instead of using toxic glues which make
it impossible to recycle them. Another approach is to design the joints
of the products – such as screws or pins – to be visible design elements
instead of hidden details. This approach requires a lot of rigor in terms of
balancing out functional and aesthetic elements into one product. A good
example of this approach is the Ago table by Alfredo Häberli for Alias.
The different construction elements of the table are designed as visible
parts showcasing rather than hiding the joints where materials converge.
This design approach uses different materials on different parts not only
as an aesthetic element but also as a construction/deconstruction process. According to the designer "his table concept is based on a pared-
down steel frame whose purpose is to secure the legs and support the
top. A supporting structure similar to a backbone, allows for an extremely
stable and visually light composition."

Material Design Drives Product and Form

There are a number of products where the functional and aesthetic properties of a material provide at the same time form, function, colour and finish of a product. This holistic approach to design does not consider CMF design as a separate discipline but instead, integrates it into the design process to create smart product constructions. This approach is also known as "materials-lead design" because the process begins by exploring the properties of the material first, according to the targeted design functionality. In the end product, the material influences the form and the form is fully supported by the material.

A very interesting example of this design approach is the Membrane chair by Benjamin Hubert for Classicon. This lounge chair comprises a lightweight steel and aluminium framework with a stretched 3D woven textile mesh. The chair weighs only 3 kg. The chair stems from the studio's materials-driven, process-led, industrial design approach, and research into the construction of tents and sports products with a focus on space frames and stretched textile. The chair utilizes a CNC-shaped stainless steel and aluminium framework to describe its shape. This framework is then wrapped in a 3D woven textile with integrated padding. The cover is secured to the framework with a series of zips and fastenings. The combination of the metal frame and padded textile allows this chair to use a minimal amount of polyurethane foam (a conventional armchair would be covered almost entirely with foam) and thus reducing the carbon footprint.

Photo courtesy of Benjamin Hubert

The Membrane chair by Benjamin Hubert for Classicon is a good example of a materials-lead design process.

MATERIAL DESIGN BASED ON SUSTAINABILITY

Thinking in terms of lifecycles – how products will be assembled, used and later on, discarded – greatly influences the selection and combination of materials.

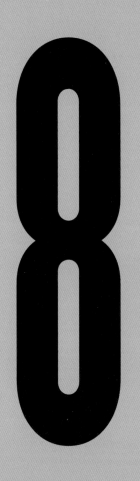

SUSTAINABLE MATERIAL DESIGN WITH THE BMWI SERIES

Using new materials and discovering more sustainable processes, can change the entire design approach as well as the final product.

Outline Structure

In the BMWi series, the innovation involves many aspects including the selection of new materials with their corresponding manufacturing processes and the design of new construction methods. As a result, this approach is now the basis for the creation of a completely new visual and functional design language, which is influencing the future of automotive design altogether and redefines the meaning of performance, efficiency and lightness. Most of its body is made of Carbon Fibre Reinforced Plastic (CFRP). The interior space is optimized and opened up, creating airiness, a reduction of unnecessary elements and a feeling of spaciousness.

During recent years, an interesting shift in the perception of surface finishes for premium automotive interiors has emerged. Traditionally the finish of materials was expected to be perfectly even and totally smooth – both to the eye and to the touch – in order to guarantee the signature

Detail of the carbon fibre structure of the BMW i3.

quality of the brand. This approach implied that the surface quality from product to product had to be replicable in mass production. However, building a product completely from scratch - as in the case of the BMWi sub brand - provided the opportunity to rethink these concepts while introducing a new appreciation for materials both from a structural and from an aesthetic perspective. By utilizing more natural materials and finishing processes, the interior surfaces yield higher surface grain irregularities, creating a feeling of uniqueness, from one product to the next.

Wood Trim

Key aesthetic characteristics of wood include the great variety and uniqueness of growth grains and textures and the way it naturally changes patination and colour as it evolves and ages. In traditional automotive interiors, wood trims are often covered with a thick, translucent layer of glossy resin, which protects the surface from scratches and from transformations caused by external elements such as, water, light and heat. This approach to creating traditional wood trims for automotive interiors is very industrial and standardized.

Detail of the wood trim on the dashboard of the BMW i3.

In the BMW i3, the natural characteristics of wood are highlighted and emphasized in the dashboard trim made from Eucalyptus – a renewable resource harvested 100% from responsible forestry. Here, the use of natural substances for the finishing process help protect and at the same time display the wood's natural aesthetics and properties, including the possibility to develop interesting patinas through time. A dark wood filler is applied to accentuate the natural contrast of grain tones. This approach to designing implies that, instead of forcing the wood into traditional industrialized processes, a process was created to enhance the material's unique aesthetic and natural properties.

Leather

Traditional leather tanning processes for automotive interiors focus on achieving consistency of quality by ensuring that the thickness of the material is the same throughout, the surface is regular and free from blemishes and the colouration does not present any major variations from piece to piece. This is often achieved through the process of chrome tanning, which produces consistent results but tends to be very toxic.

Furthermore, in order to obtain hides of the finest quality without surface regularities, they need to be sourced from places where the bulls are rarely exposed to insects, avoiding scarring and bite marks. These requirements often apply to high-end or premium applications of automotive or aviation interiors and make the price of producing premium-quality hides very costly.

What makes the leather approach for the BMWi series interesting from a materials design perspective – besides the fact that it has been organically tanned with olive leaf extracts – is that it creates a shift not just in how leather is processed but also, in how it is perceived aesthetically, when it comes to premium applications. The soft, comfortable and inviting look and feel provided by the natural tanning process, is reminiscent of that of a leather surface of a comfortable vintage chair. The finish welcomes slight patination through time and use, making the surfaces even more special.

Kenaf Fibres

A new trend in materials design for automotive interiors is the use of bio composites as visible design and styling elements. Utilizing natural fibers in door panels or parts, saves 10-50% of the weight of traditional injection moulded plastic derived from petrochemicals.

Traditionally, part of the aesthetic requirements for automotive interiors within the premium category are interior panels fully upholstered in leather or a combination of other high-end materials bonded or glued together and placed over injection-moulded structural parts. This results in extra weight and higher manufacturing costs.

Seat detail of the BMW i8 showcasing orange leather in composition with other interior trim elements.

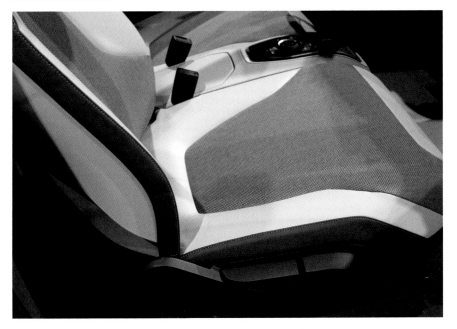

Seat detail of the BMW i3 showcasing white leather in composition with other interior trim elements.

The door panels are made with Kenaf fibres,
a renewable, raw material, and are left visible.
This decision is part of the entire CMF
composition of the BMW i3 interior.

In the BMWi series, the decision to not cover or laminate the door panels, results in reduction of weight from unnecessary layers of materials and on physical lightness provided by the use of natural fibres. Fibres from the Kenaf plant fulfil functional requirements and provide a unique take on premium aesthetic qualities. The fibres provide tactility and feelings of cosiness and closeness to nature.

The Textiles

More and more automotive interiors are utilizing upholstery textiles made from recycled content. A company called Unifi produces a sewable material called Repreve. PET bottle flakes are turned into a fiber, which is then used in fabrics. Sustainable Repreve fabrics have been utilized by several brands including Ford in their car seats and Patagonia in their high-performance fleeces. This practice, besides helping re-direct waste from landfills into products, is quickly raising consumer expectations when it comes to sustainable and functional textiles.

The fabric utilized in the interior of the i3 is made mostly from recycled polyester. This is not a natural material but it is highly recyclable, and when woven it offers a natural look and feel while providing all the technical requirements needed for high performance.

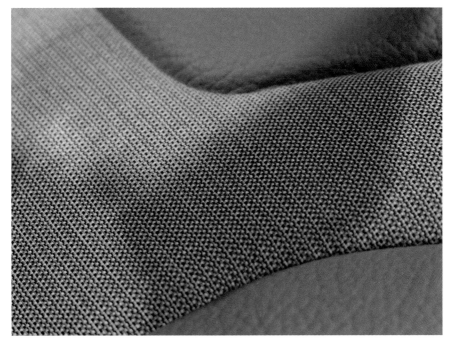

The recycled polyester textile on a seat of the BMW i3 contrasts with the natural coloured leather.

Q&A

SANDY MCGILL
LEAD CMF DESIGNER

For the past two decades Sandy McGill has split her time between Los Angeles and Munich as a lead CMF designer. Sandy joined Designworks, a BMW Group Company, in 1991 and her CMF work has been reflected in all the BMW Group brands. Her first BMW program was the colour and trim for the BMW E2 electric car, revealed at the Los Angeles Auto Show. This was followed by a stint in the BMW colour and trim studio in Munich during the development of the BMW E46 3 Series. Later she explored innovative material technologies for the BMW GINA program. Sandy conceived the colour and trim for the 2003 re-launch of the Rolls-Royce Phantom. Her work for the first ever MINI concept car debuted at the 2005 Frankfurt Auto Show. From 2003-2005, she was a member of the MINI design colour and trim team working on the 2007 MINI Coupe R56. For Designworks' external clients, Sandy has developed CMF strategies for consumer, medical and aviation industries. Moreover, Sandy designed a top-selling carpet collection for Lees Carpet. Sandy's latest foray is BMW Individual where she is working with BMW customers to design the BMW of their dreams.The many industries that Sandy created CMF designs for include transportation, consumer products, medical/dental equipment, industrial equipment, contract furnishings and household cleaning products.

How do you define CMF design?
Marketing jargon definition: A CMF designer is like a fashion stylist to a movie star but in the CMF designer's case the star is a product such as a car, a private jet interior, or a smart phone. CMF designers design and develop the colours, patterns and finishes that enliven these products.

Technical definition: CMF design is to design and develop the visible materials, which surface a product or cover a substrate.

Out of all the industries you designed for, was there a particular one where you less expected to need CMF design?

I worked on an industrial printing press that had the width of a football field – the kind that prints magazines and newspapers. The CMF design was as important as that of a consumer product. The CMF underscored the functionality, the product quality and the brand identity, which was especially important when potential buyers saw the machine at a trade-show or showroom.

Do you see a difference between the terms "colour and trim design" and "colour, material and finish design"?

Colour and trim is the traditional term for automotive colour and surface material design. For example, a car buyer chooses wheels and colour and trim in the dealership. While that term was reserved for the automotive industry, the term colour and material design referred to consumer prod-ucts. The term "finish" was added later. Now colour, material and finish (CMF) refers to designers working in a broad spectrum of industries.

I am at odds with the word "material" as it connotes material science expertise. Typically CMF designers are aesthetic, right brain types with only practical material science knowledge. The material science part of the equation is achieved through working closely with chemists and engineers. This collaboration is the most fulfilling part of CMF design – harnessing the power of science and technology with the help of experts to achieve an aesthetic vision. This may mean working with a chemist to develop a new pigment, which results in a paint with a new visual effect or a colour in a yet unachievable part of the spectrum.

Can you briefly describe BMW Individual and your role in it?

The BMW personalization program is called BMW Individual. It allows customers to create a one of a kind BMW. Through either Individual Collection or Individual Manufaktur. Customers can choose exceptional colours, beyond the typical automotive colour vernacular, offered by the Individual Collection; or a customer can give us an inspiration and we will make their dream come true through Individual Manufaktur.

I am working with BMW customers and the BMW factory to design and produce personalized BMWs. In fact, customers have the opportunity to visit the BMW Group Designworks Studio to design their personal BMW, imparting an extraordinary experience unlike any other in the lux-ury automotive market. Visiting Designworks is akin to visiting the inner sanctum of BMW Design where customers have access to the designers and design tools to create their unique vehicle. The vehicle conception at Designworks marks the beginning of the journey that ends with the BMW Welt delivery in Munich for a comprehensive BMW Experience, from conception to delivery.

What percentage of CMF is used to personalize a vehicle interior compared to other technical features?

Besides colour and trim, functional options are also available, including customized beverage coolers and seat covers for dogs.

What are essential colours and materials that instantly make an interior look and feel more premium?

Leather, and the amount of it, signifies the value of any automotive interior. Adding leather seats to a car immediately adds value. Manufacturers are strategic about how they apply leather. Base model leather packages only have leather seating surfaces while seat backs are polymer surfaces. A higher cost upgrade offers the entire seat in leather. While even further upgrades offer leather dashboards, door panels and centre consoles. Moreover, contrast stitching, piping and quilting adds value to the leather trim as it connotes craftsmanship and attention to detail.

Correlated to the amount of leather is the absence of plastic. No visible plastic is the ultimate in premium for a car, and anything else for that matter. Plastic parts can be leather wrapped. Even the smallest air vent louvers can be wrapped with leather that has been shaved to microns in thickness.

As leather becomes more ubiquitous, metal, wood and carbon signify premium. For example, the cool touch and weight of metal handles and knobs reminds us of highly engineered, machined parts, communicating superb functionality and longevity. In addition, natural wood imparts a sense of class and craftsmanship. Recently, wood has received a modern upgrade with metal details and intaglio. Moreover, carbon fibre trim has a premium sport perception as it is used on competitive performance sport cars, is an expensive raw material and is difficult to produce in finished parts. Lately, precious metal fibres are added to carbon weaves creating a luxury, sport impression.

Do the CMF selections vary according to regional preferences?

CMF selections are driven by context. Buyers choose colours based on their comfort and familiarity with colours, which is gained through exposure. For example, in heavily leafy green wooded areas like the Northeastern United States, green cars are more popular as the colour is a familiar one. In the winter time, the green car is reminiscent of the colour lacking in the natural environment. By the same token, yellow cars are popular in places where sunshine is lacking, such as Germany. On the other hand, yellow cars are also popular in places where yellow is a natural part of the environment, such as sunny climates. One is familiar and comfortable with the colour or is seeking out the colour because of its absence.

Do the CMF selections vary according to gender?

There are anthropological differences between the genders regarding colour related to hunting and gathering, but in our world today genders are relatively balanced when it comes to auto colour selections. Culture and climate have a greater effect on CMF colour preferences than gender. That said, women might veer more toward warmer, friendlier colours.

Generally, women have a big influence on car colour choices. Men will, more often than not, ask a woman for colour recommendations. A typical result is that when the car in question is an exotic sports car, a woman will recommend the car in a bright colour as if the car is the man's toy.

Are there seasonal CMF trends when it comes to making an interior feel luxurious and premium?

"Seasons" or lifecycles of cars are long: four to ten years. Car manufacturers offer editions and facelifts to add longevity to a vehicle design. The modifications always involve colour and trim as the exterior paint and leather is relatively easy to change. BMW Individual Manufaktur offered an edition of the M6 Gran Coupe with matte red exterior paint and white leather. Both finishes are valued for their perceived delicacy or vulnerability to cleanliness and wear. Adding the finishing touch while taking a cue from fashion accessories, this edition also had the Manufaktur signature emblazoned on the door sill, in the décor trim and in the leather. Branding details are also highly desirable in the luxury market.

MATERIAL DESIGN BASED ON MANUFACTURING PROCESS

Depending on the material, certain manufacturing process can be more suitable than others and offer a specific range of possibilities for the creation of form, surface finish or colour. It is key then, to explore and understand each material's own aesthetic and functional manufacturing potential.

MACHINED ALUMINIUM WITH NEAL FEAY

With expert knowledge and the right amount of creativity, experimentation and development, a material's intrinsic properties can become an integral part of the design process, fuelling the creation of truly unique results.

Neal Feay, a company based in Santa Barbara, California, was founded by Neal F. Rasmussen in 1945 during the post-World War II aluminium boom. The company is a pioneer in the creation of high-end and sophisticated aluminium products. Their innovative manufacturing processes include selected multi-colour anodizing NFS and several refined techniques for machining and working with aluminium.

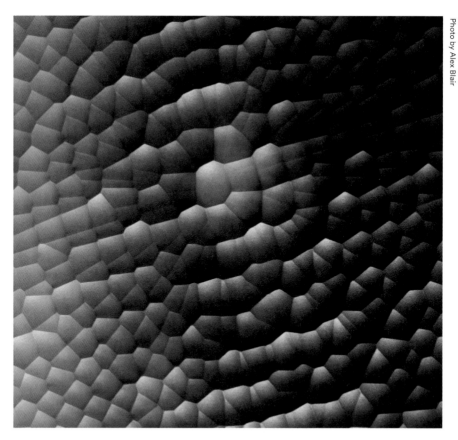

Photo by Alex Blair

The CNC milled pattern with ball end mill is followed by a selective anodizing process using water based dye. Surface by Neal Feay.

Working with Aluminium

A key principle of designing with aluminium is understanding what is possible to achieve based on how the material behaves both technically, through mechanical engineering, and practically, through industrial design.

"We never work in a vacuum, we always think about the finishing, before we work on the form. We never come up with a shape and try to figure out how to finish it or how to make it, because we are controlling the entire process, we have all of those little pieces of the puzzle."
Alex Rasmussen, President Neal Feay

Inherent characteristics of aluminium itself, such as luminosity, reflectivity, visual richness and physical lightness, yield a range of specific look and feel properties that are unique to the material. In the same manner certain finishing processes are directly related to the way the material is manufactured. For example, only pure aluminium can be anodised so if the base aluminium is not completely pure or if it has been cast with other alloying elements, it will not anodise properly and the colour and finish of the final surface will be altered. In the case of Neal Feay, a highly pure grade of aluminium is utilized for machining an initial slab which can be sheet, plate, or extrusion.

Photo by Alex Blair

Machined aluminium tray with intriguing volume and surface texture. The form and pattern were CNC milled and followed by a polish and black anodize. Design by Alex Rasmussen, Neal Feay (Design Miami 2014).

The textures on the machined aluminium wine chillers are engraved in varying depths and are inspired by the wind patterns of cold fronts as they move around the globe. Designed by Joe Doucet, crafted by Neal Feay.

Photo by Alex Blair

Different processes can be utilized to transform a solid piece into a beautiful object with unique form, surface and finish. Machining aluminium – a core expertise of Neal Feay – is a very reductive process, which usually begins by taking solid stock of the material and cutting it away with the appropriate tools. The selection of the right tooling for each form is directly related to the surface texture and therefore to the desired finish of the product or part.

"A lot of what we are doing with the surface texture is not a separate step from the form, it is completely integral to the form, so the way we create the surface, is the way we create the form"
Alex Rasmussen

When a part is machined, it will automatically display the marks from the cutting tool that was utilized to create it. These marks or steps need to be blended out later on, especially if they visually create an un-finished surface, which is too distracting or too reflective. Heavy circular machining marks for instance, create a sort of "optical illusion" surface effect and make it difficult to appreciate the form. In these cases, post-machining processes like sand blasting or bead blasting can be used to smoothen the surface and blend out tooling marks, making it less reflective and the form more prevalent.

The real genius of Neal Feay Company when it comes to materials design, lays in the creation of the entire tooling process, in order to produce beautifully refined surface textures that become at the same time finishing elements and in some cases, final products. A big part of the innovation in the tooling process has to do with what is affordable at different levels. There is a direct correlation between machining time versus cost of making a part. The key is to balance out the time needed to create a part with enough surface richness, in a way that is proportionate to the final cost. In general, the more refined and smooth the machined

Photo by Andrew Zuckerman

The (RED) Desk was designed by Marc Newson and Jony Ive for Bono's RED charity auction by Sotheby's in 2013. One of the many reasons why the desk was so unique and expensive to make is that many of its parts, besides being machined out of a single block of aluminium, were polished and finished by hand. The desk was produced by Neal Feay Studio.

texture is, the longer it takes to create it but the less post-finish treatments it will require. It is important to note however, that a surface with a refined texture is still much cheaper to make than a polished surface or a surface with no texture at all. Highly polished parts are hugely expensive to make and are much more time consuming as they involve intense hand polishing and handcrafting.

"There is a balance between how smooth we make a surface and how long it takes to smooth it out. We look at how much machine time versus how much finishing time, because we control both."
Alex Rasmussen

Texture and Form

When it comes to working with material and texture alone, aluminium is the perfect material as it is very sculptural and allows for purity of form. Since the machining of aluminium can influence the form and the surface texture at the same time, the creation of surface effects that are part of the form offer unique and very interesting possibilities of design.

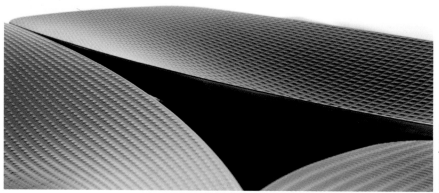

Photo by Alex Blair

Designed by Frederick McSwain and milled from solid blocks of aluminium, Lift is a series of containers that utilize texture, form, and colour to induce a visual sense of movement. Changing with the viewer's perspective, the syncopated pattern acts as a refractor of light, creating an optical illusion that rises and falls. Produced by Neal Feay.

The form of the Squircle mirror was emphasized and enhanced by letting the actual machining passes be clearly visible. Designed by Holly Hunt Studio and produced by Neal Feay.

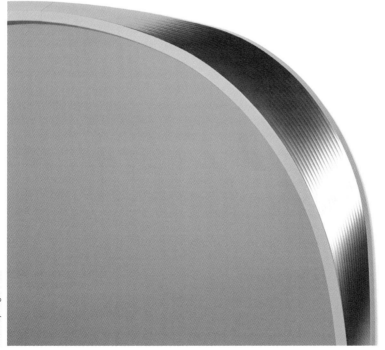

Photo by Angie West

Finish and Form

A material finish can be used to enhance the form of an object. Aluminium offers are rich variety of finishing possibilities beyond machining, which are essential to create interesting contrasts between surfaces of the same material. This is an important consideration when creating different areas of interest in products made out of a single material.

Colour and Form

Inherent aluminium colour processes, like anodizing, work directly with the soft and reflective nature of the material, and if the process is also right for the form, it will help enhance nuances and details that would not be visible otherwise.

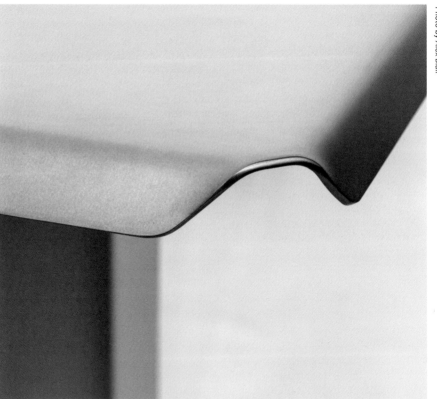

Photo by Alex Blair

The polished detail on the edge of the table was inspired by the edge of high-end leather bags which is often left visible creating a nice trim detail. Although it was possible to change the colour too, it felt more appropriate to have a polished trim as a contrasting surface detail. Design by Alex Rasmussen, Neal Feay.

Photo by Alex Blair

The half polished, half matte effect was achieved by CNC milling the form, bead blasting half of it and machine-finishing the other half and lastly, grey anodizing. Produced by Neal Feay.

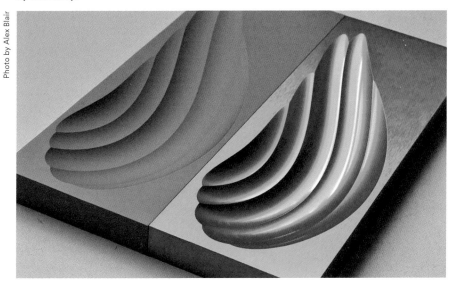

Photo by Alex Blair

The volume on the left was CNC milled, followed by one bead blast pass and grey anodizing. The volume on the right was CNC milled, followed by one pass of machine finish and teal anodizing. Produced by Neal Feay.

SURFACE DESIGN BASED ON PRODUCT STRATEGY

In some cases, product innovation lies within the design strategy of the material itself, thus influencing branding, production methods and ultimately cost.

10

MERGING SURFACE DESIGN AND PRODUCT STRATEGY WITH ROHI

Based in Bavaria, Germany, rohi is a family-owned company that specializes in locally developing, designing and producing premium quality wool fabrics. Their client list includes major airlines such as Emirates, Lufthansa and Singapore Airlines, and furniture manufacturers such as Knoll International and Vitra.

The company uses exclusively premium wool to weave seat cover fabrics as some of wool's natural properties include stain resistance, water repellence and fire retardancy. Because of these inherent characteristics of the material, there are no additional finishing processes applied to the final product other than carefully washing and drying, as well as singing its surface in order to make it as smooth as possible.

A Personalized Experience

The company's creative design team questioned why an aircraft cabin should have the same pattern on every seat, instead of offering a more personalized experience to individual passengers. They also questioned how they could create an individualized seating experience while still offering the benefit of a visually cohesive and harmonized cabin.

They setup to fully understand the design implications and technical considerations of designing a collection based on this premise. This process required an extensive level of competence and knowledge on aspects such as the different elements and structures to be combined into one layout and the selection of the right textures and colours to be used correctly in order to create and convey the idea of a cohesive yet eclectic cabin design.

Despite facing important challenges, such as higher time input into the design process and a higher level of complexity during the testing of the different visual and structural textures into a full repeat, the creative team came up with a truly innovative textile concept and a new approach to designing textiles for aircraft cabin interiors.

"The innovation delivered by rohi is an extra-long design repeat, which is composed of varying patterns, textures and styles that are strung together endlessly and transition-free. Each seat dress cover is cut from the same repeat pattern and features just one part number, reducing wastage and complexity."
rohi

Repeat

The repeat provides a design which is up to 6 meter long and is composed of several different patterns, textures and styles that are strung together endlessly and transition-free. Once the textile is woven, pieces are then cut out of the roll and sewn into dress covers, showing random sections of the repeat. Since each of the seat covers features an individual segment of the fabric design, they can then be distributed throughout the cabin in any order and, although every seat has been given its "own" identity, the overall cabin appearance remains harmonized.

"The use of a random cut-outs also allows maximum application of the fabric ensuring low wastage, reducing its environmental impact. Additionally, the random dressing of the seats with covers featuring only one part number ensures easier logistics for airlines, which also benefit from lower costs."
rohi

This design approach is interesting as it touches upon an important design strategy for CMF design, which is the process of thinking in terms of systems and product collections, rather than individual products. Product collections support the creation of series of different products that together, belong to the same family. Product collections can be unified by the design strategy or by the consistent use of colour, material and texture, providing the benefit of product variation and personalization while maintaining a cohesive design language and brand identity.

Photo courtesy of aca-3d.com

rohi next generation UNIQUE.   **rohi next generation LUX.**   **rohi next generation LITTLE.**

137

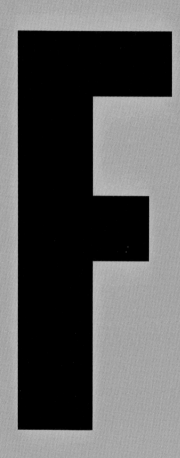

Finish Design

SENSORIAL FINISHES

There is a great variety of material finishing process. All of them, beyond their technical properties, have a sensorial aspect that helps elevate the intrinsic value of a product.

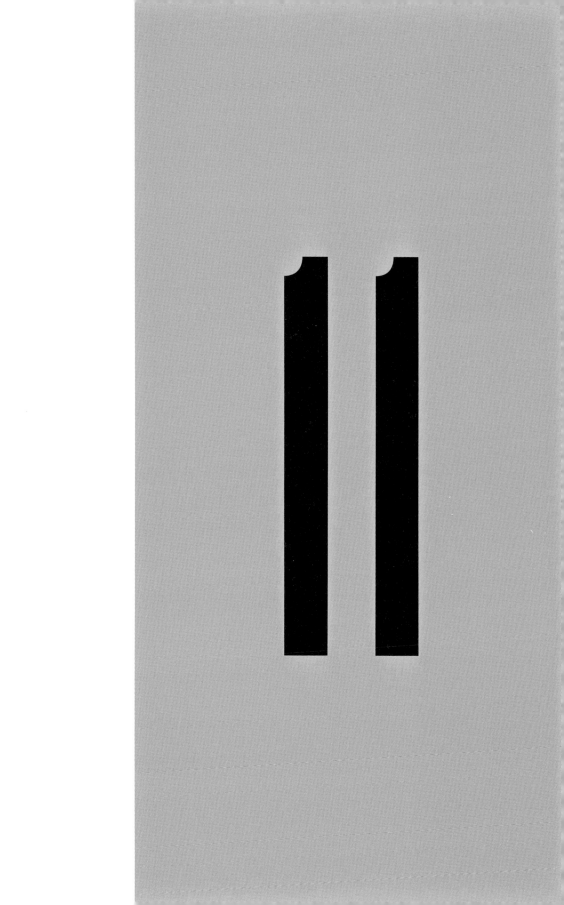

ELEVATING VALUE

The sensorial aspect of finish design is closely, though not exclusively, connected with time-intense manufacturing processes, high levels of intricacy, complexity and unique know-how. Extreme detailing makes products also more expensive as they take longer to be crafted and are more difficult to replicate.

Hand-made

Handcrafted objects are unique from the moment of creation, as they can't be exactly replicated. The skills to create hand-made products are rare and difficult to acquire nowadays. In fact, the increasing amount of mass produced consumer goods is causing many traditional manufacturing skills to disappear as the few people who had them, move out to major cities in search for better jobs. It is difficult for younger generations to take on the task to learn and preserve traditional handcraft skills without proper support from the government or the private industrial sector. Because of this, the value of hand-made products has skyrocketed within recent years, especially if it involves legendary materials or traditional making processes.

There has been an emergence of creative incubators, brand-specialized workshops, accelerators and company-run education centres promoting new education models that prioritize the preservation of skills and the fast tracking of funding for real impact ideas and enterprises. There has been a surge in the use of natural materials, such as wood, ceramics, glass and silk, in industrially manufactured consumer products, as an approach to bring back natural imperfection to otherwise overly smooth and perfect glossy products.

Wearing in

Natural materials like wood, certain metals and leather, are expected to wear out through time and usage. This property is of high value in the Western culture. Many products created with these materials – like watches, fine jewellery and classic furniture pieces – are designed to become iconic pieces and last a long time as they are handed down from one generation to the next. The materials are expected to develop some kind of "patina" and become softer to the touch as they wear in.

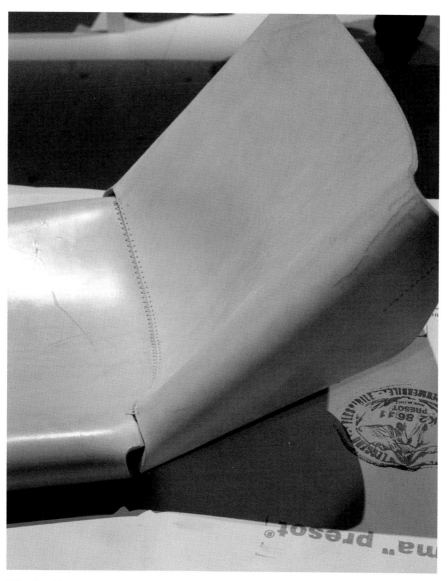

Kristalia's hide chair 1085 edition is made from
timeless materials including a natural leather
hide, which is expected to work as an evolving
canvas. It will move, change colour and develop
ageing patinas, thus becoming increasingly
more beautiful and more unique through time.

FUNCTIONAL FINISHES

Decoration technologies allow for the creation of a great variety of surface finishes, while providing materials and products with new functional qualities.

12

Q&A

NANCY HOLMAN
CMF DESIGNER

Nancy Holman is a Colour and Materials -CMF designer, most recently with vehicle design company Faraday Future. For over five years she worked at Tesla Motors as Design Manager for CMF, and was part of the core design team that helped build the multi-award winning Model S. Holman believes that her time at Volskwagen/Audi trained her well, sharpened her design skills, and gave her an understanding of what it would take to build a CMF department and lead a team at Tesla. Shortly after leaving Tesla, she was tapped by FF to help build their CMF department and launch their first vehicle. While part-time at FF, in a consulting capacity, she is stepping outside automotive industry to pursue building an on-line platform.

What are the three most common materials specific to CMF design for automotive interiors?
Leather where the finish is dependent on the materials final use. Plastic where the gloss level and grain varies depending on the zone it is used. PUR/PVC, which are low gloss and grained according to both the zone used and the appearance target.

What are the main finishing processes for each of these materials?
The finishing process for leather consists of a basecoat, which acts like an adhesion layer, much like in a paint process. It is then given a colour coat, which is typically sprayed on with automated spray guns. The final finish, the topcoat, is what provides the leather with the haptic (the touch of it) along with the grain and the gloss level, which can be low or high, depending on the initial target, as well as aid in colour fastness (how quickly the colour will fade or not fade). The topcoat helps determine whether the haptic is either dry or wet. Some OEMs (Original Equipment Manufacturers) prefer a dryer hand when touching the leather. They believe this is a more sporty approach and aids in keeping the driver from slipping back and forth in their seat. Other OEMs prefer a wet hand, which feels either wet or slippery when touching the leather.

They perceive this as a softer haptic and therefore more luxurious.

Plastic can take many forms: from soft to hard, sheets, textiles, skins or laminates, etc. For hard plastic, such as a PC-ABS or ABS, a grain typically helps to reduce light reflections on its surface, as well as provide abrasion resistance and better wear and tear. The sunlight reflecting on the top of a dashboard or shoulder of the door helps to break up the light bouncing off of the surface and reduces the reflection on the windscreen, thus providing better visibility.

The finishing process for PUR/PVC is not unlike leather. It is a very similar process, but the start is entirely different. Whereas leather is a natural material, a PUR or PVC textile starts its life out in a powder form and chemicals are added to create it in a roll form. To achieve the colour on the material, it is finished with a basecoat and lacquer is then applied, followed by a proprietary topcoat. Like leather, the topcoat helps provide the hand or haptic of the material, along with the selected grain.

Why is this process necessary for the particular material, part or function it is applied to from a CMF design perspective?

From a CMF perspective, the way a leather hide is finished is first based on the end objective. If it is the desire to present as natural a material as possible, with little to no processing, then an aniline leather is suitable. The natural markings and follicles of the hide are far more visible, there is no surface treatment to the hide, the hide is not UV stable and is susceptible to oil and fingerprint markings as well as a host of other ingredients that can readily stain and mark the hide. If however, the main objective is to significantly reduce costs, while still maintaining a leather surface, wrapped or trimmed, then a corrected grain leather, where the natural grain has been removed, is heavily coated with pigments and polymers after which a uniform grain pattern is embossed onto the hide.

Grains are a great way to finish a plastic, they provide function, visual interest through contrast between a smooth and textured surface, as well as contrast in gloss level. Gloss, like grain, can be functional, aesthetic or both. For example, a designer may want to draw attention to a particular detail or emphasize a form. This can be accomplished with gloss alone and/or texture, by highlighting one area with high gloss and the surrounding areas or details in low gloss.

The way a PUR or PVC material is finished can sometimes depend on which area of the vehicle the material will be applied to. From a CMF perspective, the finish offers the opportunity to either create a sophisticated and luxurious feeling on a door armrest, or help to cover scratches and markings by choosing a more aggressive grain for a high wear-and-tear zone.

Can you name products in the market that have this particular finish process?

You need not look any further than the fashion industry to see the many accessories and clothing items that utilize leather. The suppleness seen and felt in leather used for fashion stands in stark contrast to what is often experienced in a vehicle. This is due to the fact that the automotive industry has far greater testing and quality management processes that a material must adhere to. Coatings in fashion can be far less heavily applied, but they still run through a similar finishing process.

The consumer electronics industry has a wide array of plastic on display, from cell phones to dishwashers and TVs. Pretty much every consumer good has plastic in it. Many phones have a subtle grain applied that is hardly visible to the eye, but can certainly be felt. It is there to improve your grip.

Several high-end luxury handbags mainly consist of PVC with trimmed accents, such as a leather handle. It is also a useful and popular material in home upholstery, as it is seen as a lower costs alternative to leather, has great wear and is easy to clean.

Every material has its own set of applicable finishing processes and technologies. The more we know about how a material behaves, the more we can leverage its functional properties to create intriguing, innovative and functional finishing effects.

The construction of the wall tile includes three layers: the top "combination marble" and the middle "line gradation" have a partial matte finish and the bottom layer is done through impression vacuum metalized process.

Product and image courtesy of Nissha Printing Co.

Product by and photo courtesy of Nissha Printing Co.

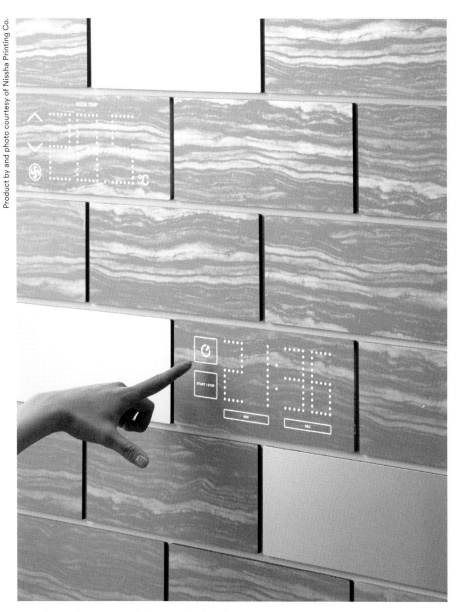

Wall tile combines In Mould Decoration (IMD) processes with panel and touch sensor technology. The touch sensor sets on the backside of the panel and the IMD uses special non-conductive ink - radio waves free - for the touch sensor. On the main surface, the printed texture and pattern resemble that of a marble tile and once it is touch, a hidden image emerges to indicate different functionalities.

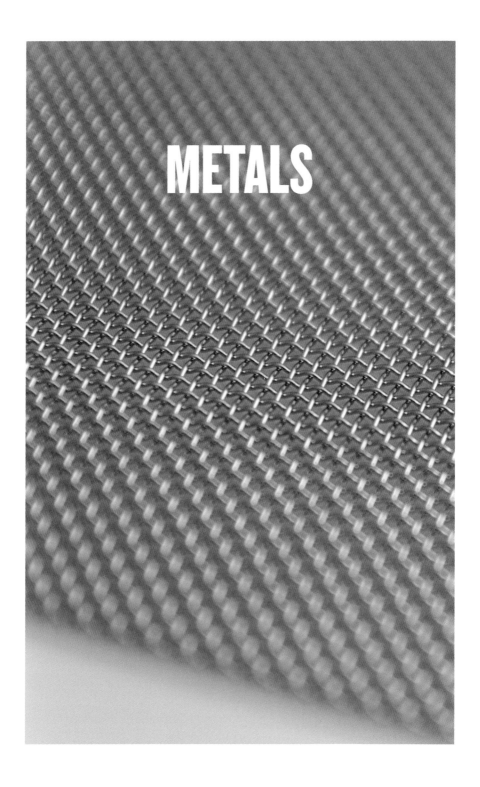

METALS

MOST COMMON TYPES

Our civilization was built based on seven metals known as "metals of antiquity": gold, copper, silver, lead, tin, iron and mercury. Currently there are 86 known metals but before the 19th century only 24 of them had been discovered.

Metals are very valuable because of their versatility, so much that products in the market with visible parts made out of metal are considered more valuable and prestigious. As metals provide excellent rigidity and durability properties, they have the highest likelihood of all materials to hold their intrinsic value over time, even after surfaces have worn out due to prolonged use.

In recent years, there has been an enormous amount of technologies developed with the scope of "simulating" metal or creating a "metallic feel" in order to provide added value to products and to scale up the price tag. Some of these technologies are plating, vacuum metalizing with metal foils and films, as well as a large number of surface finishing coatings and paint effects.

Silver
In the past, as payment for English cattle, East Germans compensated the British with silver coins dubbed "Easterlings." The Easterling became

Printed metal surfaces emulate woven and other delicate patterns. Patterns can be printed over metal surfaces with different finishes – brushed, satin finished and polished – in order to create intriguing surfaces.

widely accepted as a standard of English currency and its name was abbreviated to "Sterling," which is now used to refer to the highest grade of silver metal, indicating that it contains at least 92.5% of pure silver. Sterling silver is the whitest of all of the precious metals and has been heralded for centuries for its highly lustrous finish and versatile applications.

Silver is embraced by the medical community and by the contract industry for its antimicrobial properties. Although titanium is well known for its strength and inert qualities, other metals like copper and aluminium are also beginning to gain recognition for their antimicrobial and biocompatibility traits.

Silver, as most metals, has very good electrical conductivity properties, which make it ideal for applications such as printed circuit boards in mobile phones, computers and TV screens. Silver-based inks can produce RFID tags (radio frequency identification) used in millions of products to track inventory and prevent theft. In the automotive industry, basic functions like opening the power windows or adjusting the seats are activated through a silver, weave-conductive membrane switch.

Stainless Steel

Stainless steel is a steel alloy with a percentage of chromium content. It is used in cases where the strength and anti-corrosion properties of steel are required at the same time. Within the medical field for instance, stainless steel is used in surgical tools because of its high resistance to wear, corrosion and because of its anti-bacterial properties.

Stainless steel is a very strong material that although it is hard to form, retains its shape for a long time. In consumer electronics, stainless steel is used both for strength and for cosmetic reasons. Some of the main frames of premium mobile devices where circuit boards and display components are eventually mounted, are made out of forged stainless steel; but since the consumer usually only sees the external parts, additional finishes are needed, including brushing or sandblasting depending of the desired effect.

Aluminium

Raw aluminium is the third most abundant element on earth. Since it is a soft metal, like platinum and gold, it tends to dent and scratch easily, requiring special finishing processes and careful handling. Aluminium is the one of the most used metals in aviation because of its strength, lightweight, formability and versatility of finishing treatments such as anodizing and plating. Currently, the automotive and aviation industries are innovating through the creation of aluminium chassis reinforced with carbon fibre.

Alloys

Metal alloys – which are normally composed by two or more types of metals – are excellent when it comes to achieving specific material properties, such as improving strength while still being lighter in weight than metal itself. Some examples of metal alloys include bronze, pewter and brass.

In some contemporary products, specially in fine gold jewellery, alloys with 18-karat gold are engineered to be at least two times stronger than gold itself and to create special colour hues like rose gold for instance. Currently, some high-end consumer electronics and wearables are creating their own range of metal alloys with specific material compositions and unique shades of colours.

Photo by Brian Paschke

The BlackBerry Passport smartphone has a stainless steel structure, which also works as a frame band and as part of the main antenna. The frame wraps around the entire outer edge of the phone in a solid piece of steel, providing a solid feeling to the handset.

MOST COMMON FINISHES AND PROCESSES

There are different finishing processes which are commonly applied to metals for a variety of purposes, including the creation of surface decoration, minimizing reflectivity, improving hardness and resistance to wear, preventing corrosion, adding a colour effect and in general, all the treatments that focus on extending the useful life of metals. Below are the most commonly used finishing processes, as they relate to CMF design.

FORGING

Forging is a metalworking manufacturing process where a metal piece is compressed between two forms into a specific shape and in a controlled, uniform way to produce a very strong part. Forging can make a metal piece stronger than an equivalent cast or machined part because, as the metal is shaped during the forging process, its internal grain becomes continuous throughout, making the metal piece much stronger.

Benefits
1. Currently the industry of digital watches, is utilizing cold forging processes for stainless steel alloys, in order to increase the hardness of the material from 40 to 80 per cent and to make it more resistant to scratches.
2. Cold forging is an ideal process for soft metals like aluminium, since the material is deformed under its crystallization point. Since this process requires very little finishing work, it also helps reduce production costs.

Challenges
1. When hot forging is used, there are risks of achieving less precise tolerances and a varying metal grain structure. Also, there is a possibility of warping of the material during the cooling process.
2. After forging parts, which are both structural and cosmetic – like a mobile device chassis that is also the frame trim – the visible parts need to be polished or brushed by hand afterwards in order to create a pleasant surface finish.

CNC MACHINING

An automated program called computer numeric control machining (CNC) is utilized to achieve very high level of precision in metal surface decoration.

Benefits

1. Since CNC machining is a very accurate process, it helps decrease the amount of material waste thanks to the optimal use of the raw material.
2. It is an ideal process for fine details like grips, screw holes and other assembly features that require a very high level of precision.
3. Since the process delivers high consistency from part to part, it is ideal for high production, high efficiency manufacturing and finishing runs.
4. CNC machining is also used in low production parts as a cost efficient process that does not require the creation of moulds or tooling.

Challenges

1. Depending on the tool that is utilized to cut the metal part, the process can leave marks on the surface of the metal, which are normally smoothened out afterwards, in order to minimize reflectivity and in order to create the desired surface effect.
2. When a part is machined for a smooth polished surface quality, it requires higher tolerance and more time to machine – versus machining an intentional texture designed to utilize the milling marks as part of the final design.

Photo by Alex Blair

Milling of the Suzuri Series of table and bench seats. Design by Alex Rasmussen, Neal Feay.

Surface with machining traces.
By Neal Feay.

Photo by Alex Blair

CASTING

Casting is a process that consists on converting molten metal into a pre-existing shape or form by pouring it into al mould. The most used metals for casting include steel and a variety of aluminium, copper, iron and platinum alloys. There are different casting processes for metals including die casting, which forces molten metal into a mould normally made out of steel or zinc and sand casting, which uses sand as the mould material so in some instances, patterns are carved directly into the sand.

Benefits
1. Metal castings tend to form more precisely than ordinary forged and welded parts.
2. Die casting is an ideal process for high production runs and although it requires the creation of moulds that can be costly to produce, it yields lower production costs.
3. Die casting produces parts with very good surface finish and with good dimensional consistency throughout the production run.

Challenges
1. Although sand casting is a less costly process than die casting, it can yield parts with low fidelity to the original design.
2. In terms of surface finish, there are properties that are difficult to control such as porosity, in which case additional grinding or polishing is recommended after casting.
3. When it comes to smaller or more detailed pieces, casting may not be the most ideal process as sometimes, it is challenging to create a mould that allows for proper and exact tolerances.

EXTRUDING

Extrusion is a process, not limited to metals, in which a material is pushed or pulled through a customized die or mould. Some of the metals commonly extruded include aluminium, which is the most common, as well as brass, copper, led, tin, magnesium, steel, zinc and titanium. Besides the shape, temper and type of alloy needed, the biggest contributing factor to colour and finish during the metal extrusion process is the temperature as it provides specific hardness and finish characteristics to the material.

Benefits
1. The parts formed through extrusion processes present excellent surface finish and increased material strength.
2. This process allows for the creation of parts with very complex cross sections – with hollow cavities – enabling the use of materials that normally are very brittle.

Challenges
1. When extruding aluminium, lower extrusion temperatures can produce shapes with better quality surfaces, however, since higher pressure is needed for the process, this can be a challenge for extruding certain shapes.
2. When excessive temperatures and speeds are applied through the extrusion process, tearing of the metal can occur especially at thin edges or sharp corners, creating weaves and twists in the final shape.

CHEMICAL ETCHING

This corrosion process is used to produce complex surface decoration on metal parts with high level of detail. Chemical etching is used to manufacture intricate and highly precise metal parts with tight tolerances for different industries including aerospace and medical. The decoration in chemical etching is done by applying a layer of a selective coating, which works as a mask, and submerging the part in baths of temperature-regu-

Eco-Etch patterns for architectural applications on stainless steel by Forms+Surfaces®. Etched patterns are applied to stainless steel using an eco-friendly photolithographic bead-blasting process instead of acids or other toxic chemicals. Top: Tidal™ pattern with Seastone™ finish. Bottom: Flicker™ pattern with satin finish.

lated etching chemicals. The chemicals then react with the material dissolving it in the non-masked areas and thus creating a surface or texture effect. There is also an etching process based on photochemical etching, which is utilized to produce high precision, flat metal parts by exposing the previously laminated part section with a photo resistant coating or mask to ultra-violet rays.

Benefits
1. In this finishing process, no heat is involved – contrary to laser marking – so there are no risks associated with excessive heat application.
2. Extremely thin metal can be treated through photochemical etching without creating any distortion of the part. Neither properties such as hardness, strength or formability are affected during the process.

Challenges
1. It is a slow and a multi-step process, including the application of a mask over the parts to be treated which can elevate the costs of manufacturing.

POLISHING / BRUSHING
The process is chosen depending on the desired functional and aesthetic requirements of the external metal part. Polishing is used for mirror-like surfaces, sand-blasting for satin to matte surfaces and brushing for unidirectional satin surfaces. All those processes are performed before assembly. In premium or high-end products, the polishing procedure is often performed by hand.

Brushed aluminium is a very common trim used in several industries including automotive, consumer electronics and large-scale home appliances, providing visually appealing surface with a long lasting finish. Both, polished or sand blasted aluminium trims have become a symbol of high-end consumer products.

Benefits
1. Brushed surfaces can hide more defects and irregularities than polished surfaces. They can also withstand more wear and tear marks caused by use.
2. Brushing as well as beat blasting, are processes used to create the so-called "satin finish", a distinctive trim for metal surfaces that is not matte, nor glossy. When a satin finish is layered with colour tints, it creates beautiful colours with intriguing highlights and reflections.

Challenges
1. Brushed surfaces for automotive trim applications must be smooth to the touch.
2. In the automotive industry, tests must be performed to ensure the treated metal surface is not going to be affected by reactions to external chemicals, such as sunscreen lotion or oil from fingerprints.
3. High gloss polished metal is the most critical finish for automotive interiors applications in general because, if the surface is too reflective, it can create dangerous glare to the driver.
4. High quality surface polishing is often performed by hand, which is very time consuming and results in higher production costs.

EMBOSSING

Embossing is a process that combines heat and pressure, in order to create a tri-dimensional pattern, which is pressed on sheet metal, by passing the part through male and female roller dies. Aesthetic applications include home appliances, architectural panels as well as, automotive and consumer electronics trims. The process can be applied to different metals including aluminium alloys, brass, steel and zinc.

Benefits
1. The process of embossing allows for maintaining the same metal thickness before and after the part is treated.
2. It can be used from medium to high production runs and also for unlimited amounts.
3. It allows for the creation of unlimited pattern possibilities, which can be printed with no variation from part to part.
4. Functionally, it can help reduce friction and static of the part as well as increase its stiffness and rigidity. I can also help improve surface grip, weather the part is handheld or used for high-traffic applications.

Challenges
1. Embossed surfaces can accumulate dirt or oil through time and use, within the creases that the pattern forms.
2. Metal trims for automotive are usually no more than 2 mm thick, so patterns with extreme radios can break the part.
3. Embossed patterns can be more expensive to produce because a pattern cylinder needs to be custom-created for each design. This cost should be factored into the cost of the final part.

The aluminium trays are hand-dipped in water-based dye, a process that resembles that of painting Easter eggs. Trays by Neal Feay and Opening Ceremony.

Photo by Alex Blair

ANODISING

Anodising is a process used to make metal less affected by environmental factors, such as air and water, by increasing the thickness of the natural oxide layer on surfaces and parts. Aluminium alloys are anodised to increase corrosion resistance, allow for colouring, improve lubrication or adhesion, and to create a non-conductive layer. The most common anodising process, with sulphuric acid on aluminium, produces a porous surface which can accept dyes easily.

Benefits

1. Anodised aluminium can be up to 50% more durable than aluminium on its own. This is thanks to an anodising process that uses an electric charge and a diluted acid bath (15% per cent of sulphuric acid solution activates the anodizing process) to create a layer of oxide on the surface of the metal.

Challenges

1. Although the number of dye colours is almost endless, they tend to vary according to the type of base alloy utilized, making them difficult to replicate.
2. Anodising is the most expensive of all of the processes used to colour aluminium. Only pure aluminium can be anodised so the purity of the material is very important. Cast aluminium for instance, contains additional elements like silicone, copper and zinc, which are not evenly spread and do not etch properly. When anodised, these elements turn grey or black, producing surfaces that can be too porous to obtain the desired colour. Therefore anodising is most effective when applied to pure aluminium, preferably extruded or machined.

LASER CUTTING / MARKING

Laser cutting is a process utilized to cut different materials – including metal – for industrial manufacturing applications through the use of a high-power laser operated through optics. This process burns the material, leaving an edge with very high quality surface finish. Laser marking and laser engraving are processes more common to the jewellery and small accessories industry. While laser marking is an annealing process, involving heat treatment to change a metal surface's colour or to create a surface decoration effect, laser engraving consists of removing material from the surface.

Benefits

1. In consumer electronics, smaller and fine details like grips, screw wholes and other precise assembly features are performed by laser cutting in order to obtain a level of maximum precision.
2. Laser marking is a chemical and residue-free process, which can last longer than traditional engraving decoration.

Challenges

1. In some cases, a high amount of concentrated energy applied to a very thin part can break it or distort its form. Also, if the laser heat is not properly calibrated, burning marks can occur.
2. In general, laser markings or engravings on soft metals are likely to

scratch and wear faster than if applied on harder metals. The use of harder metals is recommended, as they are more likely to provide the surface decoration with a longer lifespan.

PVD COATING

PVD stands for Physical Vapour Deposition. It is a method where coated ions are bombarded onto the surface of a material in order to create a metallic, decorative look in a wide range of colours. PVD coatings are established surface finishing processes for the watch industry and in general products where long time quality is expected.

Some of the most common metals used in this process include, zirconium, titanium-aluminium alloys, chromium and niobium as well as brass and zinc. Depending on the industry and on further processing methods, different formulations of the PVD coatings can be created in order to elevate certain material and surface properties.

Benefits

1. Compared to traditional electroplated coatings, PVD coatings can provide higher hardness, resistance to wear and friction.
2. The process allows for a great variety of colours, which do not change or tarnish over time or under UV radiation.
3. Since the process is controlled by and stored in computer-controlled systems, the quality of the colours and coatings can be easily replicated.
4. Currently, there are new developments of hybrid PVD coating technologies and Nano-composite coatings based on a dielectric matrix with embedded metallic Nano clusters, which besides offering increased durability, will aid in the creation of new colours, like green and red, which were previously considered challenging to achieve.

Challenges

1. This process is limited to conductive materials or surfaces that can be oxidized.
2. Surfaces that have been PVD coated tend to reveal fingerprints and scratches easily.
3. If a PVD coating is used to create graphics, it tends to be more durable when applied to harder materials.
4. Because PVD coatings are very thin – 0.3 microns – when used for decorative surface finishing processes, they do not offer substantial corrosion protection to the part therefore, they need to be applied over a corrosion resistant nickel or chromium coating. In some cases, a ceramic coating is deposited during the process to increase hardness.

PLATING

Commonly known as electroplating, the process uses an electric current to ad a metallic layer onto a surface in order to impart it with physical properties such as corrosion resistance, durability, hardness and ease of cleaning. The process puts a negative charge onto the metal part before dipping it into a solution with positively charged metal ions. Due to the positive and negative charges, the two metals attract each other forming a uniform layer. There are different types of electroplating processes including copper plating, silver plating and chromium plating. The traditional plating process involves initial steps, such as polishing

Plated finishes samples by HighTech finishing.

the raw material to a mirror smooth finish, applying a base of copper to seal the surface and applying a layer of nickel to provide a durable foundation. Only after these steps are conducted, the selected plated effect can finally be applied in a polished, satin or matte finish. The entire plating process may take up to 50 steps and certain variations can occur due to poor base material quality, type of finish selected and other processing variables. Some of the most commonly used materials that get electroplated include aluminium in the aviation industry for its strength, lightweight and formability properties, as well as steel, zinc and plastics, which are widely used across industries including automotive, cosmetic package, fashion accessories, toys and a broad range od consumer electronics.

Benefits
1. This technology is very useful when it comes to providing ordinary surfaces with an elegant metal look and feel at a low cost.
2. Besides providing a wide variety of colours and textures to choose from, plating is also used to improve resistance to corrosion and wear, as well as to impart electrical conductivity to the materials or parts it is applied to.
3. It is a repeatable process, so damaged parts can be reworked to match the original existing part. This is an especially good advantage when designing large aviation interiors.

Challenges
1. Although plastics have become more popular as a base material for plating, they are often problematic due to limitations in the process and due to poor surface quality.
2. If Nickel is used in the process, additional testing for nickel release of the plated part should be conducted, in fact, for parts meant to be in direct contact with the skin, nickel-free plating processes are recommended.
3. For the aviation industry, most plating finishes are created to meet strict ISO controlled processing standards and each part needs to pass through various levels of inspection with a near zero defect ratio.
4. Satin finishes require extra steps to produce the satin lines or "grain" on the finish. Parts must be plated to a polished finish first and then a rough pad is used to manually go back and forth along the part to apply pressure to the finish, producing the satin texture. A great deal of hand skill is required to keep satin lines straight. It may take several passes with alternating pads of various levels of roughness in order to achieve the desired surface texture effect.

PLASTICS

Sensitile Systems. Photo by Dice Yamaguchi

MOST COMMON TYPES

Plastics are both synthetic and semi-synthetic materials that can be moulded into different shapes and products. Most plastics are petro-chemical based and some of them are partially natural.

The first completely synthetic plastic was Bakelite and was invented in 1907. In 1933, polyethylene was discovered. The First World War's improvements in chemical technology led to an explosion in new forms of plastic and mass production began between the 1940s and 1950s.

In today's industrial landscape, plastics are considered the quintessential material of mass production, not just because of their versatility as they offer endless creative design possibilities all throughout their production process, but also and especially because of their ease of manufacturing, their accessibility, abundance and affordability.

During the peak oil era, plastics have acquired a slightly negative connotation for being synthetic materials derived from petrochemicals. Although they have been increasingly associated with environmental pollution and waste creation; different biodegradable formulations of more sustainable plastic composites are now being developed, including bio-composites and a range of natural plastics called bio-plastics.

For CMF design purposes, plastics facilitate the offering of multiple colours and surface effects without necessarily incurring into new moulding or tooling costs. They can be coloured and textured directly in the mould. Moreover, different material effects can be added to the pigment mixture itself during its fabrication in order to achieve different looks. Metalized or pearlescent particles, reinforcing fillers and minerals or metal capable of improving plastic's performance are just a few.

After plastics are formed they allow for a broad range of post-moulding finishes such as electroplating, painting, coating, laser-marking, digital and silk printing. They are also ideal when it comes to the creation of complex forms and challenging constructions achieved through mixed processes including co-moulding with rubber or silicone, rotor moulding and injection moulding.

In terms of challenges, recycling can be difficult for certain types of plastics, such as PVC (Polyvinyl Chloride) and vinyl. PVC releases dioxins during and after its production, which may pollute the air as it produces VOC's (volatile organic compounds) which, can cause respiratory issues and headaches. The disposal process of vinyl is also challenging as it does not biodegrade; it can only become smaller and smaller through physical disintegration, so its particles can be harmful to the bodies of birds and fish.

Thermoplastics

This category of plastics requires heat to be formed. Some examples of thermoplastics are polycarbonate (PC), polyethylene (PE), polyethylene terephthalate (PET) polypropylene (PP), polyvinyl chloride (PVC), polyester (PES), polystyrene (PS), polyamides (PA) and acrylonitrile butadiene styrene (ABS).

Thermoplastics are mostly used in industrial applications and consumer products as they often provide multiple possibilities for CMF design. Some of the most common applications of thermoplastics are textiles and fibres (PES), soft drinks bottles (PET), electronic equipment cases or external package for electronics (ABS), eye glasses, lenses and baby bottles (PC), bottle caps, appliances, car bumpers (PP), synthetic leather and synthetic laminates (PVC) and car interior and exterior parts and portable mobile devices (PC/ABS).

Bioplastics

Bioplastics result from the combination of both renewable biomass (starches, cellulose, biopolymers, etc.) and fossil-based carbon. Some of them are biodegradable and therefore, used for disposable items like cutlery, vegetable containers and most recently, they are being used also in non-disposable applications such as mobile device cases, carpets and isolation for car interiors.

Plastic Composites

This category includes combinations between plastic and other materials with different physical and chemical properties, such as wood, carbon fibre, Kevlar and glass fibre, in order to produce a final "reinforced composite" with improved characteristics, which vary depending on the application. Some of the most common include, fibre reinforced polymers (FRP), carbon fibre reinforced polymer (CFRP) and glass reinforced plastic (GRP) among others.

Elastomers

These are a type of copolymers or a mix of polymers, combining both thermoplastic and elastomeric characteristics, like plastic and rubber, for instance. Thermo plastic elastomers (TPE) include thermo plastic polyurethanes (TPU) as well as other thermoplastic copolyesters and polyamides. TPEs provide products with very good tactile characteristics such as smoothness and warmness to the touch.

MOST COMMON FINISHES AND PROCESSES

INJECTION

The process of plastic injection moulding is very common and widely used in the world. It consists of creating plastic parts by injecting the heated liquid material into a previously created mould.

Benefits

1. This process is consistent, quick and accurate. Since moulds can be custom-made and also accurately repaired if they get damaged, there is a low degree of error during the manufacturing process.
2. Once the tool is created, it is possible to use different materials, colours and visual effects within the mix, in order to obtain endless possibilities.
3. If recyclable plastics are used, it is possible to grind up the waste that is produced during the process and utilize it again, so the process is very effective in terms of efficient material usage.

Challenges

1. The initial tooling costs for customized designs can be high, depending on the complexity of the part, so before setting on a specific pattern or design, it is important to ensure it will have maximum manufacturing potential and design possibilities.

Hexagonal plastic plates GE.

2. There are some limitations in terms of wall thickness, especially if the design is expected to be formed into a single part with varying thicknesses.

TEXTURE

Textured plastic can provide and elevate decorative, technical and functional characteristics of a product. There are international industry standards for moulded textures in plastics, used to clearly specify different levels of surface graining. There are also several methods to create textured plastic including, injection, thermoforming, compression and blow moulding.

Plastic textures for CMF design provide endless opportunities in terms of colour, gloss level and grain. Moulds can be custom made in order to create anything from completely polished surfaces, to leather imitation textures that create an aesthetically pleasing feel, or very coarse and rugged grains targeting high-performance applications.

In automotive interiors, the selection of textures varies depending on the zone where the material is utilized and on the targeted market tier. By utilizing a grained texture, the character and story of the design can be transferred to the product. Off-road cars for instance, will have a more robust-looking plastic texture grain, which relates to the story of ruggedness, outdoor and adventure.

Benefits

1. A textured surface can help hide the flow marks or what is commonly called "tiger skin" which results from adding decorative particles into the mix flow. Normally these marks appear near the flow gates, following the movement of the mix.
2. A grained surface will make the part more scratch resistant than a polished part. It will also provide it with better usability and ergonomics in functional areas such as grips, buttons or handles.
3. A textured plastic surface can be very cost effective in comparison to paint, as only one production step is needed in order to provide the surface's look and feel as well as a wide range of gloss/matte levels.

Challenges

1. When the moulded textures are too coarse, they can accumulate dust and dirt in more obvious ways in which case, the use of more neutral plastic colours is recommended.
2. In terms of manufacturing process, a textured mould can be more useful and practical than a polished mould when releasing the part out.
3. When plastic is mixed with special effects, special attention needs to be allocated to avoid flow marks during the moulding.

OVERMOULDING

Plastic injection overmoulding, also known as co-moulding, is a process utilized for combining multiple thermoplastic materials within a single product part. The process consists on fusing the materials together by using separate plastic injection moulds during the process.

The most common soft materials that are normally moulded are thermoplastic elastomers (TPE) and urethanes. The hard materials range from polycarbonate (PC) and some polyamides (Nylon) to some types of acrylonitrile butadiene styrene (ABS).

The most common applications of overmoulded plastics include medical devices, grip handles, appliance knobs and many domestic consumer products.

Benefits
1. Since the process combines different material properties within the same process, it is very cost effective as there are no post-assembly steps required, such as bonding, welding, painting and coating.
2. The combination of TPEs with more rigid materials provides products with a soft touch feel while enhancing its ergonomics, strength and dimensional structure.
3. In this process, the colour, material and finish emerge instantly and directly from the mould and, since the colour is embedded within the material itself there are no concerns about its durability; it won't scratch or peal like paint or other post-process coatings.

Challenges
1. When plastic is used for co-moulded parts, in production, scrap material generated by the process is commingled and fused together, making it very difficult if not impossible to recycle.
2. In use, co-moulding plastic with other materials makes repairing a single product part impossible, prompting the discarding of the entire product.
3. In disposal, recycling is ruled out due to the contamination of the material stream with different foreign materials.

IMD* - IN MOULD DECORATION

This process is used to bond a pre-printed surface or film, through injection moulding onto other parts or components. IMD is an ideal technology to create small and medium-sized parts such as control panels for consumer electronics, home appliances and direct product applications in cosmetics, packaging and automotive interiors.
Parts created through IMD are sometimes called "soft plastics" because they are made by texturing or printing a flexible and thin foil first and later

back-forming it within a more rigid material. When the foil is textured, a roller with an endless negative grain is used, which creates a positive image of the pattern on the final surface.

Currently a number of NMT (nano moulding technology) processes are also emerging to combine metals like aluminium, magnesium, stainless steel and titanium with hard resins through the moulding process. *IMD is a registered trademark or a trademark of Nissha Printing Co.

Benefits
1. IMD is one of the most versatile and cost effective methods for manufacturing and at the same time decorating durable plastic parts. It is ideal for mass production runs, as it provides highly predictable outputs with very good quality and quick turn around.
2. This process offers an endless variety of surface treatments and looks 3. from solid colours and graphics to translucent window displays – all within one single technology. Some smartphone parts are currently layering up to seven foils with different micro patterns in one single surface, in order to create intriguing tri-dimensional effects.
3. Through the creation of IMD parts, it is possible to combine functional elements such as logos, nameplates, written instructions and illumination effects together with decorative graphic elements, simplifying and shortening the production process.
4. The decorative effects obtained through IMD can closely emulate other materials and processes such as electroplating, silkscreen printing as well as paint and coating effects with equally good surface quality.
5. When NCVM (non-conductive vacuum metal) film is used, it provides a metallic surface effect, which does not interfere with antenna performance, a particularly important characteristic for digital smart devices.
6. IMD supports the creation of highly complex product geometries.

Challenges
1. Some of the limitations of IMD technology are related to the process of selection and matching of colours to other product parts, especially those made from different materials. Some pigments such as white for instance, are very translucent by nature, so certain shades of white are inherently difficult to achieve. In some cases, an additional layer with a metallic or mirror foil can be placed in between the plastic and the final foil surface, in order to create some opacity and to accentuate the desired colour effect. The colour of the moulded plastic, which goes underneath the film, can also be used to accentuate the end colour. In general, lighter shades of plastic will yield brighter and more vivid colours, in the final surface.

IMR – IN-MOULD ROLLER – IN MOULD RELEASE

In this process, the in-mould forming film is shaped and then moulded onto a plastic material through injection-moulding or pressure-casting so that the finished product is obtained after it is released from the mould and the outer base layer is removed. Trimming process may be applied to the shaped in-mould forming film before injection moulding or pressure casting.

The main difference between IMD and IMR is that when IMR is used, the final product does not have a protective film layer on the surface as this is separated from the part after the pattern or design is transferred to the moulding material in the injection process.

Benefits

1. This process is extremely cost-effective and since it has a high degree of automation, it allows for an unlimited range of surface patterns and colours.

Challenges

1. Since the final product surface is not a layer of transparent film as the film is just a carrier agent during the production process, the printed decoration can wear off or fade sooner than a part created through IMD.

Texture gradiation. Partial matte printing effect achieved through IMD technology. The matte ink sets between the release layer and the hard coat layer. After the IMD moulding process, the carrier film comes off and the matte ink defuses the light reflection as it contains some "roughness particles".

Impression VM (vacuum metalizing) effect achieved through IMD technology. This printing technique uses a clear patterned ink layer. The vapour deposition layer coincides in the gravure printing process with the pattern layer, so that an irregularity of reflection is seen on the surface of the solid shape.

Partial VM (vacuum metalizing) effect over a surface with a printed wood texture. The entire effect is achieved through IMD technology.

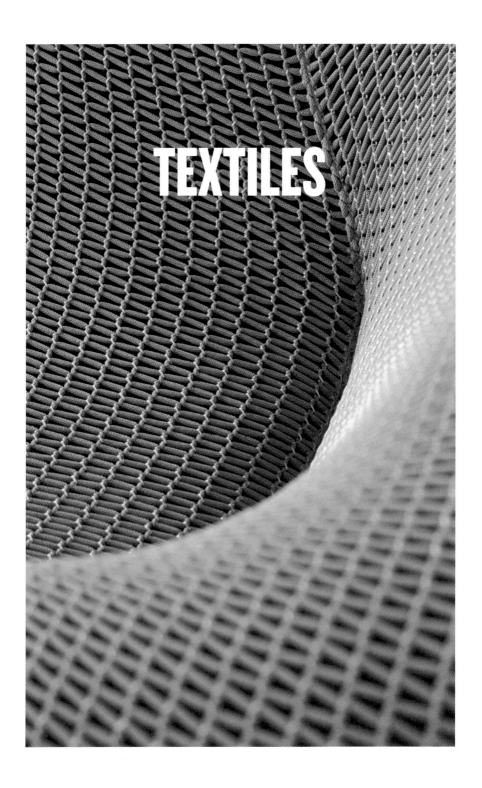

TEXTILES

MOST COMMON TYPES

Textiles have existed since mankind's instinct was to seek and to create shelter and protection from the elements by weaving materials. Since then, the use of textiles has been ubiquitous and connected with a sense of comfort and wellbeing.

Today, the level of technology involved in the creation of textiles is quite amazing ranging from Nano materials to "programmable" textiles that change colour and respond to digital and electronic commands, revolutionizing the smart wearable device industry.

Textiles are also ideal for CMF design because of their unique ability to combine functional and aesthetic properties. From the decorative point of view, there is a broad range of post processes, when it comes to creating multiple variations of the same product range and personalizing alternatives, including printing, heat bonding, perforating, laser, stitching and embroidering.

From the construction point of view, fibres with different properties can be woven or layered to form structurally sound surfaces and support very specific functional requirements. For instance, layered textiles can confer sound absorbing properties to products or, when a material like wool is utilized to construct the fabrics, it will provide it with low flammability and high adaptability to changing climate conditions.

In CMF design, textiles are utilized by a number of different industries ranging from interior design, automotive, aviation, medical, soft goods (apparel and sports), and most recently the growing industry of wearable electronics. For every industry, textiles must fulfil specific technical and performance requirements. In aviation and automotive for instance, they must meet international safety standards and regulations as well as functional properties such as water repellence, flame retardancy, good resistance to abrasion, light and colour fastness, excellent breathability and good moisture transport.

In automotive interiors, textiles are mainly used for upholstery, door panels and headliners and the main focus is on combining properties such as acoustic isolation, sustainability, high performance, comfort and ease of care. Some of the most common finishes applied to fabrics for automotive interiors include, anti-static, anti-stain, weather-resistance, water proof, and anti-bacterial. Depending on the type of performance requirements for every vehicle category, the finishing processes applied to textiles will vary.

There are many different types and ways to classify textiles for which we would need to create an entire new book. In general, they can be classified under the type of materials utilized: natural, synthetic or both, under the type of fabrication process: woven, knitted, layered, bonded, tufted, non-woven, etc., or under the types of decoration treatments: printing, lasering, embroidering, stitching and so on. For the purpose of this book, we will list a few of the most commonly used types and treatments, as they support CMF design, below.

MOST COMMON FINISHES AND PROCESSES

KNITTING

Knitted textiles are created through a system of loops, which are formed and interwoven by a single thread. They are ideal for sportswear and apparel as they are flexible and can be constructed in small or large pieces depending on the need.

There has been a surge of all-knitted sportswear where different types of construction weaves are interlocked together to form the entire upper of the shoe. These types of structures utilize only one strand of ultra-strong yarn to form the entire textile construction, making the final product very lightweight and adaptable to the shape and movements of the wearer's foot. This type of constructions, especially in the footwear industry, help eliminate unnecessary glues, adhesives and material combination mixtures that are difficult to recycle.

Benefits
1. By knitting, it is possible to build tubular or tri-dimensional constructions, which are ideal for apparel and sport applications that need to form around the body's contour.
2. Knits structures are based on interlocked loops, which provide products with stretchable properties, ideal to tighten and snug around irregular shapes.
3. Most types of knitted constructions, especially meshes, are often wrinkle resistant due to the flexibility of the weave.
4. Knitted mesh textiles are also more breathable as the technical construction of the weave forms a porous surface that is ideal for products requiring the circulation of air or ventilation.

Challenges
1. Because of their less stable structural composition, knitted fabrics tend to stretch and shrink constantly as a response to applied forces, this may cause less structural stability – compared to woven textiles – unless they are bonded to a more stable substrate.

The upper part of the Nike Flyknit Racer is formed by a
seamless knit upper. The technology was originally inspired
by runners who wanted the combination of the snug fit of a
sock combined with lightweight and versatility.

2. Knits are by nature porous constructions with irregular surfaces which may present challenges when it comes to water and wind protection.

BONDING

Bonding textiles is a process where two or more layers of woven or non-woven materials are formed together to behave as a single material. The most traditional textile bonding process occurs between textiles and foam which is common within automotive and aviation soft cover uphol-stery, commercial and residential furniture, wall acoustic panels and in sports applications such as show insoles, body supports and brace wear. There are different kinds of processes utilized for bonding including ther-mal and ultrasonic bonding. The ultra-sonic process uses high frequency ultrasound weaves to molecularly bond multiple materials together – most commonly thermoplastics. It can also produce a range of finishes like laminating, embossing, perforating and cutting all of which make the process ideal for manufacturing medical, surgical and sanitary products.

Benefits

1. This process is ideal for non-woven materials as it can bring dimen-sional stability, surface decoration and a combination of functional properties to them.

2. Ultrasonic bonding can be more cost effective than other bonding processes since it does not utilize adhesive materials. At the same

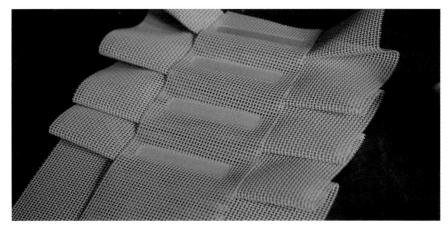

Material bonding study for the Crease and Weld
bag series designed by Joris de Groot, using
PVC and machinery to produce rain gear. The
panels are "sewn" together using a micro-
wave-like, high frequency welding technique.

time, it allows for the creation of different surface decoration patterns during the process.

3. Ultrasonic welding is a process ideal for cutting and at the same time sealing edges of fabrics which normally tend to fray, such as edge trimming of fleece material.

Challenges

1. When adhesive adherents are utilized, they must first be separated before recycling the fabrics, which can be challenging. Because of this, there is a new range of adhesives being developed called "dismantlable adhesives" with recyclability in mind.

PRINTING

There are different processes for textile printing, including digital and screen-printing. Digital printing can be applied to any kind of fabric and is based on ink jet technologies, which allow for the creation of extremely high definition, photo-realistic prints. The process is based on computer-controlled high-speed valves, which inject the colours into the surface with high precision and depth. This process can be applied to both synthetic and natural materials including wool, polyamide, polyester and acrylic.

Benefits

1. With digital printing it is possible to create and produce one-off designs or change designs on the go, as the process is based on individual valves rather than on lengthy repeats which require to change inks and rollers.

2. Digital printing offers the possibility to print unlimited colours in large formats – some machines measure up to 100 meters long.

Challenges

1. When screen printing is utilized, a repeat for mass production is needed in order to maximize the size of the pattern.

2. When a repeat is used to print the fabric, it brings challenges to the upholstery process in terms of accurately cutting and sewing the textile to match the repeat, generating the use of extra material and the creation of waste.

MOST COMMON TYPES

Leather is a durable material that comes from the hides and skins of animals including mammals, birds, reptiles and fish. After treatment, leather provides a warm and sophisticated feel with a particular tactile appearance accentuated by a natural scent.

The provenience of the leather hide, or more specifically where the animal lived, is very important in order to assess the quality of the material. Some manufacturers of high-end leather hides for aviation and automotive interiors, utilize hides sourced from Germany, Italy and Northern Europe, since these are considered, according to industry standards, to be the finest hides in the world because the bulls there are rarely exposed to barbed wire and insects so the skins don't have scarring or bite marks.

When leather is used in its many different applications, it improves the visual appearance of the product and its added real and perceived value, not only for being a natural and authentic material but also because as it ages, it develops a beautiful soft patina and a more personal connection with the user. There is always an extra premium to pay when choosing leather as an upgraded option for consumer products.

Function wise though, it is not always the best choice for certain applications. In upholstery for aviation for instance, there is a preference for textile over leather, especially for longer flights, as textile tends to be more breathable and comfortable. Nonetheless, leather is usually easier to wipe clean than textile.

The question to choose textile or leather is also cultural. European airlines are more inclined to use textiles in Premium classes for its functionality, while Asian and Middle Eastern airlines still prefer to use the natural, classic leather and to compensate for the lack of breathability, they create design solutions where the passenger does not sleep on the main leather surface of the seat but instead, on a textile surface that emerges once the seat becomes flat.

Natural leather
Natural leather is the resulting product of treating real animal hides with a range of natural or artificial finishing processes. Depending on the required application, these processes provide the leather with its final appearance and specific level of quality through factors such as smooth or coarse touch and evenness of surface irregularities as well as colour, grain, texture and surface shine.

E- Leather
E-leather is made out of natural leather scraps, which are grind and bonded to a textile backing and embossed with a grain texture. The main

advantage of e-leather is its lightweight. It also has better quality and consistency control for colour, texture and durability. Currently several aviation interior applications are moving towards e-leather, since it has the perceived value and good cleanability properties of real leather, yet it is half its weight.

Synthetic Leather

Synthetic leather, commonly known as faux leather is a man-made leather imitation. It has properties that regular leather does not have, like added flexibility or four way stretch, which make it ideal for applications like upholstered aircraft sidewall panels.

Napa and Suede

Suede leather is made from the splits of large animal hides and from the underside of the skins of calf, lamb, goat and sometimes deer. Although suede has a natural soft touch surface, which is thin and pliable, it tends to be less durable than leather with full grain or a treated top surface. Suede is ideal for some upholstery and soft goods.

Napa is a softer kind of leather that comes from the skin of young lamb and calf. Contrary to suede, it comes from full grain or corrected grain surfaces, which are also died and textured through regular processes. Since napa leather has a very soft hand, it is often used for lining the interiors of personal leather goods that are in close contact with the skin, like high quality wallets, toiletry kits, gloves or shoes.

Embossed and perforated leather targeting both aviation and automotive upholstery applications. The surface details reveal intricate woven-like embossed and laser-cut patterns.

MOST COMMON FINISHES AND PROCESSES

TEXTURE

Although leather has a natural grain, which is on the smoother side of the skin, it still gets grained or embossed artificially with different textures as a part of the finishing process. This process is done through the application of extreme pressures, and the result pieces are known as "corrected grain" leathers. There are also a few hides with a perfect natural grain texture and those are used for extremely high-end product applications. High-end brands like Rolls Royce for example, pick out only the best leathers with the best and smoothest surfaces thus eliminating the need for an additional texture finish. These are known as "full grain" leathers.

Other texturing processes such as embossing and debossing consist on heat pressing onto the leather surface with a solid metal die, creating indentations of impressions

Benefits
1. The bigger the grain structure/pattern that is engraved, the more defects and irregularities from the natural skin it will hide.
2. It is possible to create a two-tone contrast within the leather surface by dyeing the top or "crust" layer in a different colour and later on debossing a pattern onto it.
3. Textured leather and suede are used to enhance grip areas, such as steering wheels grips or seats for sports cars.

Challenges
1. Debossing or embossing leather increases its perceived and real value but it also decreases the strength of the area that gets treated.
2. In general, the more layers of finishing processes applied to a leather hide, the stiffer and less elastic it will be.

DYEING / TANNING

There are different processes to colour leather, including chromium, aniline and vegetable tanning. The most traditional process, chrome tanning, uses a solution of chemicals, acids and chromium salts. Aniline tanning is a process that uses only soluble dyes and leaves the surface without the application of any finish or topcoat. Vegetable tanning uses vegetal-based substances such as bark from trees. All processes work better when applied to good quality leather as opposed to split or bonded leather.

Benefits
1. Chrome tanning is a quick process that provides the leather pieces with a more permanent and longer lasting colour, which does not change throughout the product's lifespan. This process can also provide leather with stain and water-resistant properties.
2. Vegetable tanning produces usually warmer and richer, more natural tones as only natural ingredients are used for dying. This also allows for the leather pieces to develop interesting patinas through time and use, making them truly unique.
3. Vegetable tanning allows for fully recycling the material after used, so it is more environmentally friendly than chrome tanning.

Challenges
1. When aniline tanning is used, the final surface of the hide will reveal its natural grain as in the original animal skin – blemishes, scars – and it does not present a uniform colour surface throughout.
2. Vegetable tanning can take up to 40 days to produce, since it is mostly done by hand, which makes the final product more costly but also more special.
3. Vegetable-tanned leather tends to discolour faster and to be less resistant to water, so it tends to shrink after getting too much humidity and moisture. If submerged in hot water, it will shrink and become extremely rigid.
4. In general with any dyeing process, lighter shades of leather, especially when used in automotive and aviation interiors, are harder to clean and can get stained from external elements, like the indigo dyes from denim jeans.
5. Chrome tanning has severe environmental implications since chromium is a great pollutant and the leathers dyed through this process are difficult to recycle. Chromium-tanned leather can contain between 4 and 5% of chromium and cause allergic reactions to the skin. Recycling and re-using of this type of leather is very challenging as the chromium content in it cannot be destroyed or eliminated.

PERFORATING
Leather can be perforated in various different hole patterns. Typical applications are steering wheels and automotive seat accent panels.

Benefits
1. Perforated leather is often and mostly used for its sporty aesthetic.
2. It is ideal for climate-controlled seats as the tiny perforations also work as a vehicle for ventilation.

Challenges
1. Perforated leather is less resistant to wear and can tear around the perforated holes. Smaller hole patterns are less likely to have tear problems.
2. Dirt can accumulate within the perforated areas.

LASER MARKING / CUTTING

Laser marking consists of engraving the material surface through a sublimation process caused by a laser. By calibrating the performance of the laser and its travel speed, the depth of the pattern can be modified. Laser cutting consists of actually cutting the material with extreme accuracy, in a specific pattern or shapes. For the purpose of cutting leather, a laser cutter called CO_2 is the most commonly used as its gas beam type is easily absorbed by organic materials.

Both processes are common in the fashion and accessories industries. In automotive interiors however, laser marking is more rear because the structure of the leather can get damaged and the end surface, resulting from the marking, needs to be sealed in order to comply with high industry standards and regulations.

Benefits
1. Laser cutting can create extremely flexible, yet strong leather surfaces ideal for apparel, accessories and soft goods applications.
2. Laser cutting is also used to cut leather in an extremely precise way, avoiding fraying edges. This makes the technology ideal for decorating small accessories or to create intricate surface patterns with an almost hand-made quality at a relatively low cost. In fact, there is a growing demand for laser cut textiles in general within the fashion and apparel industry.
3. Because this is a non-contact process, the tool does not wear off and the marking of the patterns remains consistent in depth and quality throughout.

Challenges
1. Leather surfaces to be laser cut or laser marked must be completely flat, with no crises or wrinkles as these can challenge the laser beam to remain focused, creating unwanted pattern or cut distortions. Leather surface textures are equally important, the smoother they are, the best results will be obtained while marking or cutting them.
2. Laser cut edges in leather will normally be slightly darker in colour than the original surface tone, in general the thicker the leather surface to be cut, the darker the edge tone will be.
3. When laser marking a vegetable tanned leather, the marks or the

pattern tend to appear darker or more contrasting with the surface colour than if synthetic of heavily processed leather is used.

STITCH, EMBROIDERY AND PIPING

As with bespoke suits or custom car interiors, the stitching used to trim or construct the products, is key in order to impart and define the quality, look and feel of the product. Stich-finishing on leather for aviation and automotive interior components, is a skilful practice with numerous pattern and construction variations, such as plain seam, contrast stitch seam, flat seam, French seam, topstitch seam and many others.

Leather embroidering is a way to premiumize any type of leather application. In some interior leather applications, especially within the luxury sector, the embroidery is mostly custom- made and sometimes done by hand.

There are also other finishing details, like the piping of the seat covers, which is a type of trim created with a strip of folded leather, or other material in some cases. In order to create the piping the material is cut on the bias as this way, it will have more elasticity to go around different contours without creating bulk. In some cases, a tubular cord or similar insert is placed inside the piping detail, in order to create and even, fuller trim.

Benefits
1. Stitching can be used not only to construct the product together but also to create the trim detail, all in one single step, i.e. cushion tops in different colour and material compositions as part of the seat cover of automotive interiors.
2. Embroidering a logo or a custom-detail is a very elegant way to personalize it and provide it with a sense of exclusivity.
3. Piping details can be used to define and accentuate forms, material contrast and, in some cases they are used to create visually recognizable brand elements.

Challenges
1. Delicate hand stitching will naturally result in increased manufacturing time and in a higher price point. This is usually a positive element when it comes to luxury goods but it tends to be avoided within mass-market products.
2. When stitched patterns are used as a decoration element, it is important to plan how the pattern will work within the entire design of the interior where it is placed. In general, the more complex the design of the stitching is, the more time consuming it will be to make and the higher the cost.

Maserati seat with embroidered logo on the seat
headrest. The stitched seat trim detail works both
as a construction and as a decorative element.

WOOD

**Detail of Jo Nagasaka's resin and wood furniture
for Established & Sons.**

MOST COMMON TYPES

Wood is a natural material with an intrinsic comfortable touch. It provides objects with an authentic feel and when combined with metal trims, it creates an instant classic look.

As wood ages, it develops a patina, an attribute that helps increase the perceived value of a product.

Currently, wood is becoming a very popular and desirable material, especially in industries like consumer electronics and high-tech products. The main reason for this surge is that natural wood brings a natural feel to traditionally and otherwise cold-looking tech applications, providing them with a unique and authentic finish – as natural patterns are always different – and making them fit better into warmer home environments.

Natural Wood
Natural wood from trees is increasingly considered a vital material to support the natural ecosystem. There has been lots of controversy about the sustainability level of natural wood products recently, especially when it comes from endangered species, therefore, certain types of wood are now harvested from renewable resources and the creation of designs is based on specific wood life cycles.

Natural wood can be broken into two main categories, solid wood (lumber) and veneers. Veneers are thin layers of natural wood cut from a log, cut either rotationally around the log or directionally across the log. The cutting direction is used to describe the wood figure of a veneer, for instance flat cut has a large cathedral figure while quarter cut and rift cut have a straight figure.

Since wood is a natural material, it tends to absorb moisture and expand or shrink depending on environmental conditions. Different types of wood applications require different coating and finishing processes in order to stabilize it before it gets laminated onto other substrates and also to provide it with new functional and aesthetic properties, depending on its final application.

Some important functional attributes of wood include the fact that it is a highly acoustic material with heat isolation properties – regardless of external temperatures – and the fact that it does not accumulate electro-static charges.

Engineered Wood
Engineered woods, such as MDF or plywood, are man-made or "composite" woods created by binding wood fibres, strands or veneers with a range of adhesives and dyes in order to create a final "engineered" product with exact performance specifications and visual characteristics

Specially processed veneers by Italian manu-facturer Tabu. The veneers are manufactured and dyed providing consistency of pattern and colour. The process yields an almost infinite range of possibilities when it comes to colour options and surface design.

Image by Dice Yamaguchi

according to industry standards or targeted applications. A large number of engineered woods are currently being developed not only as a way to preserve natural forests, but also to ensure continuity of certain patterns and grains. A high level of exclusivity can be achieved through the creation highly customized wood patterns, through very precise engineering processes.

APPLICATIONS

Traditionally, wood trims have been used in car interiors to create a personalized environment and elevate the value of the product. Initially, actual trimmers with carpenter skills were responsible for crafting automotive interiors trims, a practice that made the parts very unique but also very costly. Today high-end brands still maintain the tradition of using real wood trims by layering thin veneers, while lower-end brands have replace them with plastic films with patterns that try to imitate real wood.

Wood applications for consumer products, like automotive and aviation trims or small part inserts for consumer electronics, are created with thin veneers ranging from 0.25 to 0.8 mm that are bonded with adhesive to a less expensive core material or substrate, in order to provide them with form and rigidity and as a way to make the material more stable.

For this process, veneers are utilized instead of solid wood because although the latter one offers beautiful patterns, it is also very unstable or prune to warping and splitting. Once the wood is sliced into veneers, the adhesives added during the manufacturing process and the base substrate to which it is glued, helps control its natural movements and to present a visually appealing and functionally stable surface. The most commonly used substrates for wood veneer applications in automotive, aviation and consumer electronic industries include: fiberglass, plastic (ABS), metal (aluminium), carbon fibre and plastic-metal hybrids.

MOST COMMON FINISHES AND PROCESSES

LASER AND ENGRAVING

The laser process can be used to cut, engrave and build intricate pattern designs and wood on wood inlays. The laser marking of wood is normally done with a laser machine that uses a 1.6 microns weave length. Before the laser marking process, the part to be treated is usually covered with a film or tape in order to protect it from vapour damage and to avoid staining during the process. In some cases, after the laser marking is done, the surface needs to get lightly sanded in order to remove any unwanted dark marks occurred during the process.

To create inlays, the design is laser-engraved within the main surface. Then the same pattern is laser-cut from a different type of wood veneer and later inserted into the recessed area of the main surface created by the engraving process.

Benefits

1. Through laser marking, it is possible to achieve significant depth, as well as colour and surface contrast at quick speeds.
2. Wood types with high oil content will engrave better and produce cleaner designs with better contrast. Likewise, surfaces with tighter and finer wood grain will yield clearer, more contrasting designs.

Challenges

1. When laser marking/cutting composite wood veneers, if the laser cuts too deep into the surface, some of the added external elements like adhesives or resins – can cause unexpected burns or unwanted effects in the design. This can also happen to the edges of the part, which might burn faster and darker than the wood itself. In these cases, proper calibration of the laser speed and temperature is recommended.

2. If additional surface finishes are required for the part – such as waxing, lacquering or oiling, it is recommended to apply those before the lasering is done.

POLYURETHANE COATINGS

Although PU coatings are used in different industrial applications and on different material substrates, one of its most common applications is on wood dashboard trims for automotive, which are usually coated with a layer of polyurethane as a protectant. PU coatings provide wood parts with good resistance to moisture, chemical and mechanical impact and help to smoothen out surface imperfections. Consumer products using wood veneers, especially those expected to be in close contact with human skin, can require up to five layers of PU coating applied to their surface. Most PU coatings are either organic, solvent or water based.

Benefits

1. PU coatings provide an instant layer of isolation from external elements, protecting the parts from water, dirt and humidity in general.

Sample courtesy of KEYROU, 1Plus and Akzo Nobel

The mobile phone wood cover is made with a front and back veneer layer held together by a glass fibre layer. A conventional PU system was used for the coating by applying five layers of transparent colour in order to cover and smoothen the wood's surface imperfections.

They also seal in oil and solvents resulting from the manufacturing process of the actual wood part.

2. PU coatings are soft to the touch which provides the surface with a smooth appearance without altering the wood's essential look and feel.

Challenges

1. There is an increasing demand for water-borne and one-step application for PU coatings due to restricted industry regulations and sustainability concerns. However, when it comes to consumer applications, more natural finishing processes for wood, such as natural fillers and waxes, are being prioritized as they allow the wood to be in closer contact with external elements and therefore evolve and change with time.

DYEING

One of the most common industrial processes for dyeing wood veneers consists of impregnating the thin sheets in soluble dyes, through a process of immersion in stainless steel tanks with controlled temperatures. The colourants utilized for wood staining range from pigments colourants to dye colourants, and can be classified according to the solvent in which they dissolve: water, alcohol, lacquer thinner or oil soluble dyes.

Benefits

1. Dye-based stains are used in more refined applications like inlays or delicate veneer work as they produce surfaces with even colour since their particles are very small and penetrate deeply into the wood structure, giving it a darker and clear colour.

2. Natural and water-based dyes are more environmentally friendly as they are made with organic components and don't have toxic chemicals such as chromium or heavy metals.

Challenges

1. Pigment colourants have a larger particle and therefore do not penetrate as deeply into the wood surface as dye-based pigments do, providing a slightly muddier or less clean colour.

2. Dye stains tend to change colour over time, as they are more sensitive to UV radiation. In some markets like Europe, this is a highly appreciated characteristic while in markets like China or North America this can be perceived as poor quality. Normally though, UV coatings are applied to the veneers as a finish to protect the colour from light effects.

GLASS

The Window Glass Table by Nendo contains four layers of glass with cutout squares, creating interesting shadows and textures.

MOST COMMON TYPES

Glass is a man-made material – made mostly out of silica – with a rich and beautiful appearance, which provides a sense of quality and value. It is thought to have been made initially in the shape of Egyptian beads between 2750 and 2625 BC and yet today it is regarded as a highly sophisticated material that maintains its value through time. As this material continues to gain popularity during the digital age, it has been used as a direct metaphor to reference our current period in time as "The Glass Age".

Some of the key characteristics of glass, which cannot be re-created or surpassed even by the most sophisticated imitation material, include its clear transparency, its compressive strength and its coldness to the touch. Its transparency makes it an ideal material choice for digital displays and for interactive surfaces that require high transparency in order for the light to come through and high surface rigidity in order to protect internal parts.

Challenging physical and mechanical properties of glass, like its brittleness and heavy weight are being surpassed by incredible technological advancements, ranging from optical fibre to bendable glass panes – as flexible as paper – utilized to laminate and protect other materials and surfaces.

As this material continues to gain importance for a number of contemporary uses and industrial applications, it continues to be re-engineered for higher performance with anti-shatter formulations, layered constructions and with new treatments including anti-microbial formulations and oleo phobic, anti-abrasion, and anti-glare coatings.

In terms of more aesthetically driven processes of glass there is a very wide and almost endless palette of aesthetic possibilities, which are currently having a sort of "new renascence" as they are re-discovered by young designers and craft makers, especially in the area of home accessories and tableware. Some of these processes include tinting, metalizing, printing, laser marking, acid etching, carving and engraving.

There are in general six types or categories of commercial glass based on chemical composition:
1. Soda-lime glass, which contains from 60 to 65% content of silica and is the most common and affordable type of glass.
2. Lead glass, which has high content of lead oxide and offers excellent electrical insulating properties.
3. Borosilicate glass, which has at least 5% of boric oxide content and offers resistant to high temperature changes and corrosion.
4. Aluminosilicate glass, which has aluminium content and offers high

durability and is ideal for applications involving electrical conductivity or high temperatures.

5. Ninety-six per cent silica glass which has almost none non-silica elements, so it can resist heat-shock for up to 900 Centigrade.

6. Fused Silica glass, which is very difficult to fabricate but can withstand temperatures higher than 1200 Centigrade for short periods of time.

MOST COMMON FINISHES AND PROCESSES

TEMPERED AND LAMINATED GLASS

Since glass is very fragile and brittle, it tends to shatter on impact, producing small cracks which eventually grow into a larger cracks. In order to avoid these problems and also to increase its strength, a tempering process is usually followed. Tempered glass is treated by controlled thermal or chemical currents that increase its strength, and create imbalanced internal stresses, prompting the glass to crumble into small granular pieces when hit by a sharp object or sudden impact, making it less likely to cause injury.

As a result of its safety and strength, tempered glass is used in a variety of demanding applications, including passenger vehicle windows, shower doors, architectural glass doors and tables, refrigerator trays, as a component of bulletproof glass, diving masks, and various types of plates and cookware.

Laminated glass is typically inter-layered with PVB (polyvinyl butyral) or EVA (ethylene-vinyl acetate). Technically treated layered glass is a type of safety glass that holds together upon sharp or sudden impact, creating a "spider web" pattern. In many cases the glass layering is designed to be more ornamental as well, especially for architectural applications, where interlayered textured films are bonded between two sheets of glass.

ANTI-SHUTTER GLASS

Recent anti-shatter glass formulations are based on altering the molecular structure of glass through "ion exchange processes" where surface ion particles formed during the manufacturing are replaced with larger ion particles, in order to create compressive strength pressure and manage the required tension on the part or product. These new formulations contribute to the creation of thinner and therefore lighter glass pieces, ideal for automotive applications where lighter weight results in higher efficiency.

ANTI-SCRATCH

Traditionally in the high-end watch industry, sapphire glass is utilized, as it is highly resistant to scratches although it tends to be very brittle. Recent anti-scratch formulations of glass composites are aiming to achieve similar scratch resistance properties than sapphire glass in combination with increased breakage strength.

Anti-scratch formulations and coatings for glass in commercial applications – such as camera lenses, watches, notebooks, TV displays and smart phones – help prolong the life of products. They can be applied through different methods including thermal and UV cured, as well as through deep and flow applications and because they are compatible with anti-reflective, mirror and metalizing treatments, they are often combined to offer also these properties.

OLEOPHOBIC COATINGS

Oleophobic coatings are not limited to glass surfaces. They can also be applied to other materials like metals, polymers, textiles and glass ceramics to name a few. These coatings are normally applied on surfaces expected to have direct contact with human hands such as interactive displays of digital devices and smart phones. They are often formulated to be nano scale thin and some of them also help provide hydrophobic or water repellence protection. The most common application methods for oleo phobic coatings involve vacuum and/or vapour deposition and spray processes.

ANTI-GLARE/ANTI-REFLECTION

These types of coatings are used to minimize surface reflections, help sharpen visual contrast, reduce glare and make images more realistic by improving contrast definition. They are used in a wide variety of applications, including automotive, instrument panels, binoculars, camera lenses, telescopes and high-resolution applications such as digital art.

ANTI-MICROBIAL

With the growth of touch-displays made out of glass in digital electronics and in large-scale interactive panels, the spread of microbes has become an increasing concern. Anti-microbial properties for glass are becoming rapidly the norm, especially if they are also combined with other protective properties. The anti-microbial function properties are directly built into the glass by incorporating silver ions into the formulation, as previously noted, silver has anti-bacterial properties that naturally help reduce the spread or germs.

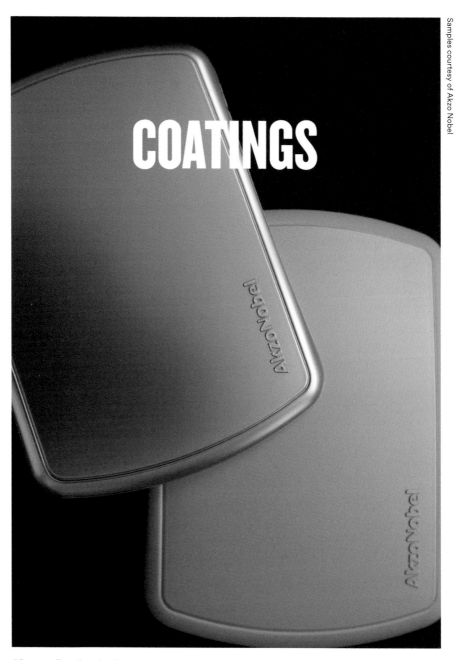

Samples courtesy of Akzo Nobel

COATINGS

After sanding the plastic, a layer of transparent coating is sprayed to cover surface defects. After the surface is smooth, a mirror silver coating is applied. Lastly, a final layer of translucent topcoat containing UV resistant elements is applied.

MOST COMMON TYPES

Coatings are a range of finishing processes utilized to improve the visual and functional quality of a surface. Besides paint, which is one of the most commonly and broadly used finishes, there are many other types of coatings which are selected and applied depending on the desired final functional and aesthetic properties of the product. Basically, any kind of improved performance or mechanical property to be imparted onto a surface can be achieved through the application of a coating.

Coatings can be purely decorative or purely functional, however, in most consumer product applications, coatings are used for both purposes. There are two kinds of general systems in the coating field, UV-based (Ultra Violet) and PU-based (Polyurethane). Currently water-based formulations involving one-step application processes are in high demand for cost efficiency and sustainability reasons.

The coatings applied during the product manufacturing process are called industrial coatings and they are the focus of this section, as they are part of the design and manufacturing process or industrial product design.

There are nuances and deep technical knowledge involved in the selection and application of final coatings involving the creation of complex multi-layered structures, capable of providing a substrate material with UV or scratch resistance and properties such as self-healing, oil repellence, water-proofing, fire retardancy, soft touch, anti-reflectivity, self-cleaning, anti-microbial and many more.

There are different stages to the application of coatings depending on the desired finish effect. One-step coatings are based on single-application systems and are considered to be more efficient and sustainable. Most coating processes however, involve two general steps: the base coat, which defines the colour and the visual effect, and the topcoat, which besides defining the gloss level and tactility of the surface, also protects the base coat.

Some special and complex coating processes can involve the application of five or more coating layers in order to create unique and exclusive effects. For these types of multi-stage processes, the first step usually consists of the application of one or more transparent layers to seal and smoothen the surface so it can receive further processes; this step is particularly common for porous or coarse materials like wood. The next step is the application of the colour and visual effect to provide the part with its aesthetic and visual characteristics. Finally, the last stage consists on the application of the topcoat layer.

In terms of chemical formulations for paints and coatings, there is a broad spectrum ranging from solvent to water-based. Within the automotive interior and the consumer electronic industries, there are new and more sustainable developments including, low temperature energy-saving coatings, which cure faster than the traditional two-stage PU coatings and can be applied on plastic, composites and/or metal substrates.

MOST COMMON FINISHES AND PROCESSES

SOFT TOUCH

In order to achieve the soft touch feel, coatings are applied as a finish onto surfaces of products from different industries including consumer electronics (laptops, phone cases, handheld electronics), household appliances (vacuum cleaners, personal care, baby products), medical and fitness devices (personal trackers, portable health monitors) and automotive interior components.

The most common application of soft touch coatings are over product parts expected to be in close contact to the touch, such as handles, operation buttons or grips. In automotive interiors for instance, soft touch finish is used on instrument panels and door trims as well as on console and steering wheel components, in order to increase the overall "soft comfort" of the space.

Benefits
1. Soft touch finishes are used to provide surfaces with a luxurious touch and feel in fact, they can transform a coating's industrial feel to resemble other materials like velvet and leather, especially if combined with a substrate surface with a pre-moulded 3D pattern in it.
2. Soft touch coatings offer very low reflectivity and low gloss level to the surface they are applied to. This is an ideal characteristic for parts and components utilized within automotive interiors where minimum reflectivity is required for safety purposes.
3. They have also become very resistant to abrasion and scratching which used to be a challenge in the past. Recently, one of the latest developments of soft touch formulations, include resistance to chemical elements like the combination of sun lotion and the insect repellent DEET.
4. Soft touch coatings can provide the possibility of creating different colours easily and they can be combined with other properties such as UV resistance, in order to provide the parts with extra technical characteristics.

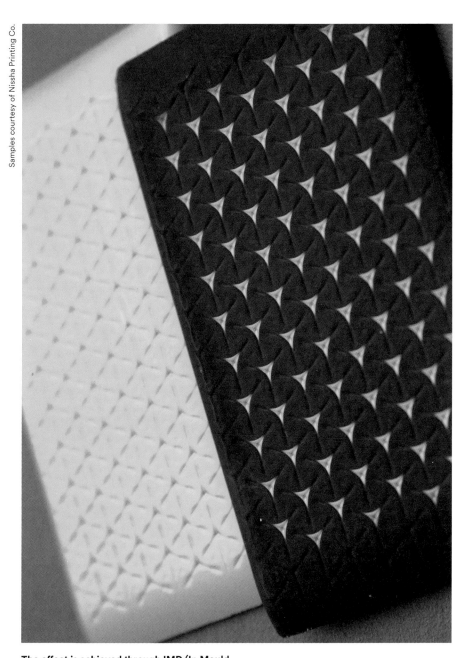

The effect is achieved through IMD (In Mould
Decoration) technology. The "baby touch feel"
is added through a coating process applied to
the IMD film. Paired with the soft form of the
product, the overall effect is very pleasant to
the touch.

A three-layers coating finish is applied on Kevlar®, a material made by Du Pont™ with aramid fibres, which has very high strength and is very lightweight. It was coated through a conventional PU coating system involving the application of four layers of transparent colours, in order to hide and smoothen any material irregularities. The first layers consist on soft touch coating followed by a polishing process. The final layer consists on soft touch coating only.

Sample courtesy of Keyrou and Akzo Nobel

5. The latest developments of soft touch coatings include water born polyurethane formulations that provide low odour and low VOC (volatile organic compounds) emissions, which makes them more environmentally friendly.

Challenges

1. Soft touch coatings tend to be thicker than other coatings such as UV for instance, so they can add some weight and thickness to the part.

2. These type of coating finishes do not bear or withstand too much dirt and cannot be wiped clean easily as the final surfaces, despite being very soft to the touch, present high texture density in micro pattern formations.

TOPCOAT

Topcoats are generally the last layer applied to a "base coat" or a substrate material. Since they have no pigment content, they tend to be of clear or translucent colour and their main function consist on acting as surface protectants and sealers, while adding specific technical and aesthetic properties to the parts.

There are several varieties and formulation of topcoats, which can be water-based or solvent-based. There are also different application methods, including air-drying which hardens with oxidation, acrylics which dry by solvent evaporation, and PU- or epoxy-based, which dry by cold-curing chemical reactions. Some types of epoxy coatings can be also cured through high temperatures, which transform them into harder finishes.

Benefits

1. Topcoats, especially with glossy finish, act visually as magnifying glass, making the coating effect look very clear and the colour more intense and beautiful.
2. Topcoats can improve the performance of any surface by adding technical characteristics to it such as scratch and chemical resistance and improved UV performance. They can also reduce moisture penetration and provide surfaces with different levels of reflectivity ranging from matte and satin to high gloss.
3. The use of topcoats make the surfaces easier to clean as they maintain external and potentially harming elements on the external surface preventing them from penetrating and damaging the basecoat or the actual substrate material.

Challenges

1. When using high gloss UV resistant topcoat, especially with a deep colour, the surface will tend to reveal oil marks from fingerprints and scratches more easily.
2. Topcoats tend to be denser in formulation than basecoats since they are pigment free and they have lower pigment to solvent ratio.

PAINT AND SURFACE EFFECTS

Surface effects a normally decorative paint finishes applied to plastic or other substrate materials, in order to give them a specific look and feel and to increase the "added value" of the final product. They can be achieved through the combination of colour, texture effects reflectivity (gloss level), base material texture, etc. Some of the most common surface effects applied through conventional spraying methods include pearlescent, metallic, magnetic patterns, colour shifting and soft touch. Other application methods can yield different surface finish effects.

Powder coating for instance, which is applied as a free-flowing powder, will yield a visually perfect and smooth surface in terms of pigment and colour distribution.

Not all surface effects in consumer products applications are generally achieved through the application of paints and coatings. When working with plastic for instance, it is possible to ad the desired effect directly into the pigment mix before the fabrication or moulding of the part. This approach can be more cost effective than post-process surface effects, as it is done in one step.

Benefits

1. Coating effects are a direct way to increase product differentiation without necessarily creating new product designs. In fact, the same product can be on the market for a longer period of time when only "seasonal surface updates" are done through unique and novel coating effects.
2. Paint is one of the most versatile coating finishes for many industries and products as it allows for the creation of an almost infinite range of decoration effects at a relatively low cost and with a quick turn around.

Challenges

1. The pearlescent finish in particular tends to be somewhat translucent due to the very nature of the pearl particle, therefore the base colour of the substrate needs to be carefully selected as it might show through or visually alter the final effect.
2. Applying a metallic finish effect to a surface can render it electrically conductive. This is a special consideration when the end use of the part is any kind of electronic equipment.
3. Not all substrates are suitable to apply paint and finish effects easily, in some cases it is necessary to smoothen and prepare the surface through grinding, polishing or even applying layers of transparent coating in order to smoothen it and cover defects. These processes are especially necessary when creating fine finishes effects like "mirror silver" which requires a perfectly smooth substrate surface.
4. Some base materials, like PP (polypropylene) require the application of a gas flame method beforehand – which supplies oxidized gas air to the part – in order to provide a chemical bond on its surface that facilitates the adhesion of inks and paints. They key is then to select the right material for the right finish or the right finish for the right material.

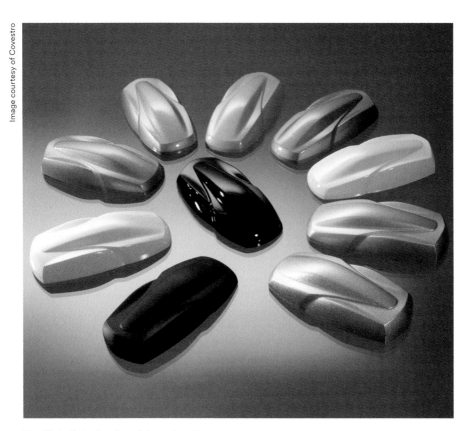

The Blulogiq technology is based on the use of a thermolatent hardener which activates at 80°C and rapidly cures the coating on the plastic substrate. The technology has the latitude to be used in most colour and finish currently offered. For automakers, this translates into a significant time and cost advantage, while also significantly reducing energy use.

COLOUR DESIGN

· Eiseman, Leatrice. *Color: Messages and Meanings. A Pantone Color Resource*. Gloucester, MA: Hand Books P, 2006.
· bourncreative.com/meaning-of-the-colorgold
· bourncreative.com/meaning-of-the-colorsilver
· empower-yourself-with-color-psychology. com/color-white.html
· empower-yourself-with-color-psychology. com/color-red.html
· empower-yourself-with-color-psychology. com/color-orange.html
· empower-yourself-with-color-psychology. com/color-yellow.html
· empower-yourself-with-color-psychology. · com/color-green.html
· empower-yourself-with-color-psychology. com/color-blue.html
· empower-yourself-with-color-psychology. com/color-purple.html
· empower-yourself-with-color-psychology. com/color-silver.html
· empower-yourself-with-color-psychology. com/color-gold.html
· empower-yourself-with-color-psychology. com/cultural-color.html
· empower-yourself-with-color-psychology-com/color-black.html
· en.wikipedia.org/wiki/beet
· en.wikipedia.org/wiki/carrot
· en.wikipedia.org/wiki/cephalopod_ink
· en.wikipedia.org/wiki/chili_pepper
· en.wikipedia.org/wiki/clitoria_ternatea
· en.wikipedia.org/wiki/clover
· en.wikipedia.org/wiki/corn
· en.wikipedia.org/wiki/gold_leaf
· en.wikipedia.org/wiki/rice
· en.wikipedia.org/wiki/vark
· informationisbeautiful.net/visualizations/ colours-in-cultures
· netlibrary.net/articles/carrots
· sensationalcolor.com
· xrite.com/fm-100-hue-scoring-system/ accessories

Allsteel Clarity Chair
· allsteeloffice.com/synergydocuments

Coloradd
· coloradd.net
· youtu.be/qbb-htbrhpi - video

Colour Discrimination Tests
· color-blindness.com

Fluorescent Colour Tests
· dayglo.com/who_we_are/fluorescent_color_ theory

Digital Colour Readers
· shop.variableinc.com/pages/colorsubscriptions
· colourpinbyncs.com/ - ncs colourpin

Zero Project - Colour ADD
Universal Graphic Code
· zeroproject.org/practice/colour-identifica-tion-system-for-the-colourblind/

MATERIAL DESIGN

BMW i3
· draexlmaier.com/fileadmin/ user_uploads/_docs/fachartikel/atzworld-wide_2014_116_06_i_020-023_kenaf_draexl-maier_onlinepdf.pdf
· bmw.com/com/en/newvehicles/i/i3/2013/ showroom/design.html

Recycled Textiles
· repreve.com

FINISH DESIGN

Anodizing
· en.wikipedia.org/wiki/brushed_metalfinish-ing.com/53/33.shtml

Bayer Coatings
· bayermaterialsciencenafta.com/newsletters/ apr15/index.html

Chemical Etching
· fotofab.com/cmp_typical.php

Coatings
· akzonobel.com/wood/ee/system/images/ akzonobel_industrial_finishing_wood_facts_ and_figures_tcm125-34902.pdf
· designnews.com/document.asp?doc _id=229027&dfppparams=ind_183,aid_ 229027&dfplayout=article

Cold Forging Process Apple Watch
· apple.com/watch/craftsmanship

Cold Forging Process Huawei
· prnewswire.com/news-releases/huaweiun-veils-huawei-watch-at-mobile-world-con-gress-2015-300043257.html

Crease and Weld Bag Studies
· fastcodesign.com/3023268/wanted/manu-facturing-materials-become-minimalist-hand-bags#1

Digital Printing
· zimmer-austria.com/en/products/products/ chromojet/chromojet-digital-en/index.html
· dailydesignnews.com/moooi-launches-newcarpets-company

Elastomers
· en.wikipedia.org/wiki/thermoplastic_
  elastomer
· glstpes.com/resources_trends_consumeren-
  hancement.php
Embossing
· advantagefabricatedmetals.com/embossing-
  process.html
Extruding Metal
· en.wikipedia.org/wiki/extrusion
· bonlalum.com/extrusion_process.shtml
Flexible Glass by Corning
· corning.com/in/en/products/display-glass/
  products/corning-willow-glass.html
Forging
· en.wikipedia.org/wiki/forging
Glass Types
· cmog.org/article/types-glass
Glass Video - How it is Made Guys
· youtu.be/12osbjwogfc - part 1
· youtu.be/13b5k_laabw - part 2
huawei ascend P7
· consumer.huawei.com/au/mobile-phones/
  gallery/p7-l10-au.htm
IMD
· nissha.com/english/products/industrial_m/
  imd/index.html
IMR
· google.com/patents/Uus20110251706
Injection Moulding Plastic
· avplastics.co.uk/advantages-and-disadvan-
  tages-of-injection-moulding
Laser
· engadget.com/2014/06/17/laser-cut-
  clothingexplainer/
· cutlasercut.com/laser-cutting-materialslaser-
  engraving-materials/laser-cut-leather
Lasering
· info.laserstar.net/blog/bid/87785/traditional-
  engraving-vs-laser-engraving-for-jewelry
Leather
· haipeichem.com/uploadfile/
  2013/1109/20131109033635111.pdf
· maxwellscottlm.hubpages.com/hub/
  chrome-versus-vegetable-tanned-leather
· leathernet.com/leather.htm
Leather Stitching
· innovationsautointeriors.com/auto-uphol-
  stery-stitching
Leather Tanning
· oecotextiles.wordpress.com/tag/vegetable-
  tanning
Metal Forging
· thomasnet.com/articles/custom-manufactur-
  ing-fabricating/hot-forging-cold-forging

NMT (Nano Moulding Technology)
· chinainmould.com/article-891-1.html
· chinainmould.com/article-936-1.html
Plastic Composites
· sciencearchive.org.au/nova/059/059key.html
Oleo-phobic Coatings
· aculon.com/oleophobic-coatings.php
· youtu.be/rR_lx9CPcao - Video 1
· youtu.be/q2b39dNjj9o - Video 2
Plastic Overmoulding
· evcoplastics.com/overmolding
Polypropylene Processes
· ineos.com/global/olefins%20and%20poly-
  mers%20usa/products/technical%20informa-
  tion/ineos_polypropylene_processing_guide.
  pdf
PVD Coatings
· pvd-coatings.co.uk/applications/decorative
· inform.pt/nano4color
Silver
· silverinstitute.org/site/silver-in-industry/
  electronic
**Soft Touch Video from Bayer Material
Science**
· youtu.be/naddif8or4q
Textile Bonding
· texbond.co.nz/products
· books.google.com/books?id=cskoekzxvl8c&
  dq=recycling+bonded+materials&-
  source=gbs_navlinks_s
Textiles - Ultrasonic Bonding
· textileworld.com/issues/2005/november
  -december/features/ultrasonic_bonding
  _of_nonwovens-films_and_textiles
Topcoats
· corrosionpedia.com/definition/1098/
  topcoating
Wood Dyeing
· awfi.org/wood-dye-stain-technologies
· alpiwood.com/en/production_process
Wood Laser Marking
· lotuslaser.com/applications/wood-laser
  etching
· boothveneers.com
· youtu.be/x4w0vuojagu
· mataauto.com/?page_id=3565
· joewoodworker.com/veneering/why-useve-
  neer.htm
Wood Veneers Manufacturer
· tabu.it
ZTE Grand S EXT (NMT)
· chinainmould.com/article-1081-1.html

CMF Design
The Fundamental Principles of Colour,
Material and Finish Design

Publisher
Frame Publishers

Author
Liliana Becerra

Research assistants
Rhadika Balla, Amaya Gutierrez,
Victoria Lin and Kristina Marrero

Production
Sarah de Boer

Graphic design
Liliana Becerra, Carlo Llacar,
Claudia Geidobler, Zoe Bar-Pereg
and Barbara Iwanicka

**Concept, production and
photography ice creams colours**
Liliana Becerra, Carmen Rosa Lopez and
Paulino Pachacama

Prepress
Edward de Nijs

Thanks to contributions of
Claudia Geidobler, Janice De Jong, Suzette
Henry, Nancy Holman, Johannes Lampela,
Angelina Li, Sandy McGill, Rick Niefield,
Hirobe Nobuyasu, Brian Paschke, Alex
Rasmussen, Natalie Roy, Stephie Sijssens,
Diceke Yamaguchi, Akzo Nobel, Clariant
Automotive, High Tech Finishing, Mold-Tech,
Neal Feay, Nissha Printing Co. and Rohi

**Trade distribution USA and
Canada**
Consortium Book Sales & Distribution, LLC.
34 Thirteenth Avenue NE, Suite 101,
Minneapolis, MN 55413-1007
United States
T +1 612 746 2600
T +1 800 283 3572 (orders)
F +1 612 746 2606

Trade distribution Benelux
Frame Publishers
Domselaerstraat 27H
1093 JM Amsterdam
the Netherlands
distribution@frameweb.com
frameweb.com

Trade distribution rest of world
Thames & Hudson Ltd
181A High Holborn
London WC1V 7QX
United Kingdom
T +44 20 7845 5000
F +44 20 7845 5050

ISBN 978-94-91727-79-5
© 2016 Frame Publishers, Amsterdam, 2016

Printed on acid-free paper produced from
chlorine-free pulp. TCF ∞
Printed in Slovenia

9876543